Mime
and
Masks

by Roberta Nobleman
illustrated by Katherine McCabe

New Plays Books, Trolley Place, Rowayton, Connecticut

*This book is dedicated
to Patricia Hale Whitton
with love and thanks.*

FOREWORD

Every child is a Mime — naturally. All households with children have been overrun with extra "Mommies and Daddies," assorted other human beings, animals, and mechanical objects from robots and escapees from *Star Wars* to cars, trains, helicopters, and airplanes. Even such inanimate objects as trees and flowers have moved indoors. What *is* this phenomenon that causes such a metamorphosis?

According to Webster's New International Dictionary, mime is "a kind of drama in which scenes from life were imitated and generally represented in a ridiculous manner; also a dialogue composed to be recited at such representations." The Random House Dictionary probably comes closer to the general public's definition of the term. It calls it "the art or technique of portraying a character, mood, idea, or narration by gesture and body movements . . . to play a part by mimicry, especially without words."

By any definition, Mime is a powerful tool, not only for actors, but also for everyone who works with children — and that is the "raison d'etre" for this remarkable book by Roberta Nobleman. For the teacher of elementary grade students, **Mime and Masks** offers a multiplicity of ideas useful in many curriculum areas; career guidance, science, language arts (literature and composition in particular), social studies (including geography, history, conservation); music, art, dance, etc. The educational novice, as well as the seasoned teacher, will find that the many exercises offer professional help rarely, if ever, found elsewhere.

Mime and Masks shows you how to use the best creative instrument people have: their bodies. Everybody can use them, including those who are non-English speaking or those labeled "slow" or "dull." The author has found these latter to be "among the most creative, the most free, much to the amazement of their teachers. What a thrill for these children to be the best at something!"

Actors of any age should find the chapter on "Occupational Mime" most helpful during early rehearsals since they must use this mime before the set arrives . . . to indicate the opening of doors, turning on a television set, or whatever action the script calls for that must be done with an invisible set or prop. In addition, there are many other ideas throughout the book to help an actor develop a character.

The segment of this book dealing with masks is unique in that it not only shows how to create masks from all kinds of materials, based on the personal experience of the author . . . its unique contribution is to show many ways in which to utilize them, rather than merely let them sit decoratively on the wall. A quick glance at the Table of Contents will show the diversity of masks included. An extra dividend is the inclusion of several mime plays, most of which also involve the use of masks.

If, as Wordsworth wrote, "The child is father to the man," or conversely, in John Dryden's words, "Men are but children of a larger growth," then just about everybody interested in creating "theatre" on any level will find something in this book to help that creativity along. While it has been written with the elementary grade teacher in mind, there are suggestions which will be useful, for example, for breaking the ice at the first get-together of a cast for either a professional or amateur company, for groups of strangers getting together for a lengthy conference, children and/or staff on their first day at a new school, club, camp, recreation or senior citizens group. Even the social scene will get ideas for theatre games and charades. The possibilities offered are stimulants for endless creative ideas for "the seven ages of man."

In the pages ahead, with their abundance of excellent, helpful pictures, you will be educated, stimulated, inspired to create and help others create . . . what? You name it. Happy miming!

Paula Silberstein
Bureau of Audio Visual Instruction
New York City Board of Education

CONTENTS

"Acting without words."

"It's when you use your body, but not your mouth."

"It's when you're climbing up a rope — but there's no rope, so you have to use your imagination."

"It's the most fun I ever had."

These are some of the definitions children give me. I do not think adults would have any better answer, because mime is not an immediately recognizable, popular art form, like music, or art, or dancing. Yet mime *is* an art form — the oldest, and the most universal.

Before Stone Age man thought to depict the story of the hunt on the walls of his cave through painting, we may be sure he had already acted it out with movement and sound. Our bodies are, quite simply, the handiest thing around for communication. Drop a versatile mime artist into the middle of a jungle tribe, or an Eskimo village, or a Chinese commune, and he (or she) will soon have everyone laughing or crying. What other art form can communicate itself so readily to *all* human beings, regardless of age, race, creed, culture, or language?

Expressive movement is a very primary force. The infant sees an object that she wants, and stretches out her hand to reach it, anouncing, through gesture, "I want that colored thing." When she cannot reach it, she will add sounds of frustration, but the movement comes first. It was very exciting when we heard the voice of Neil Armstrong speaking to us from the moon, but the image of that Giant Step, the eerie space movement — *that* said more than all the words in all the languages ever known to man.

What Mime is Best at

If mime is the first, and most universal, art form, it is because we are all endowed with the "mystical three" — body, mind, and spirit. Mime uses the body to reveal the workings of the mind and spirit. The famous mime, Angna Enters, has said, "Mime is best only for that for which there are no words, or for which too many words would be required." A critic of the famous Swiss mime troupe, Mummenshanz, has said that the mime show "puts the audience in touch with a part of themselves they had forgotten they owned." The stammered cry. . .the outstretched hand. . .the back bent low. . . the puckered lips. . .all tell more of truth than can be written on passionless paper.

Of course mime cannot convey all the details of language. Many of us have experienced the frustrations of trying to communicate with someone who does not speak our language. There was the amazing story of the young black boy who was found wandering in the streets of New York City. He spoke no language known to anyone in that vast jungle of many tongues, home of the United Nations. His gestures told tales of beatings and killings by white men, but the where, the why, the when — for these questions, he needed words. Human beings developed vocal language because the mind and spirit had too much to say — too many details. So if mime cannot say everything — and if what it does say is so elusive and elemental — how can it be of use to our children as part of their learning process?

Let me give you an illustration from my own childhood experience. I was born near London in 1941. We were not evacuated till the end of the war, so I grew up with terror from air raids at night, and the restrictions of wartime during the day. In my elementary school class there were 45 children and one teacher. The one great joy in my school life was Wednesday mornings when we were all taken down to the hall (all-purpose room), and spread out over the space, where the B.B.C. Music and Movement programs brought us the magical world of mime on the big old-fashioned radio. Now we could forget everything as we reached to the sky to pick a golden apple, or slithered along the floor like fire-breathing dragons. The music got faster and faster, and now we were huge engines, tearing through the darkest tunnel.

These were the learning experiences that stayed in my mind from those grim days when many war-torn schools had given up everything except teaching reading and writing. These B.B.C. programs, incidentally, continue today for British elementary schools.

But Isn't This Too Refined And Esoteric For American Kids?

For many people, Marcel Marceau and his appearances on television are what we know best of "the silent art." Marceau brings a very distinctive, elegant French technique to all he does. I can sympathize with the teachers who see little connection between his concentrated, often solo art form and the pack of noisy, gum-chewing, football-playing kids that make up their classes. I do not think his type of mime is entirely appropriate for the majority of children in our schools today.

There is, however, another "school of mime," in which I guarantee that in every class in your school there are at least one or two children who could easily be honorary members. I remember an Indian boy on a reservation in northwestern Ontario, explaining so vividly — in mime — what happens to animals during a forest fire. I remember a little girl in Watts, Los Angeles, doing the most accurate and amusing character study of different leaders of her community program. I remember six children in northern New Jersey who, quite by accident, found themselves stuck together like Siamese sextuplets; they then proceeded to a series of adventures worthy of the best silent movies. I remember a deaf child miming the life of a lonely old man and his cat. For this kind of mime — more robust, less obviously "arty" — perhaps the word pantomime is more appropriate.

The Difference Between Mime and Pantomime

Pantomime is generally considered to encompass a broad world of movement whose tradition lies with the clowns and comics of the theatre, as far back as the Greeks and Egyptians. In Roman times Lucian complained that all work ceased in "the Pantomime season," for everyone just sat and watched.

Pantomime embraces music, dance, acrobatics, sound, even words. We may use it as a general term to describe non-scripted theatre.

Mime is a much purer art form. Performed in silence, through a highly disciplined body — it goes beyond the level of entertainment to beauty of style — and often to abstract meaning. When Marcel Marceau performs the humorous "skit" of Bip at a *Party,* that is pantomime; when he is locked in the struggle of one terrifying cage after another, that is mime.

(In England, "Pantomime" is also a special kind of family show, performed during the Christmas season, with dancing, singing, comic routines, magic, and audience participation, all tied into a fairy tale, like *Jack and the Beanstalk or Cinderella.*)

To describe the work I do with children, I like the word pantomime. It embraces a wide range of creative movement, and its derivation bespeaks its universality. . .PAN, the personification of nature, and MIMOS, or mimicry. In Greek the word Pan was similar to the word "all," and gives the god Pan his universality PAN-TO-MIME can therefore mean the whole world at your feet. . ."all kinds of mimicry." When I see a group of children wholeheartedly responding in movement and sound, I feel the spirit of Pan, King of the Wild Country, with his horns and his hooves and the music made by the reeds of the river, is alive and well, if only we will respond to this universal call.

The Dwindling Role Of Expressive Movement

In many parts of the world expressive movement still plays a very important role in the everyday lives of people. It is a sad fact that when our mechanized world takes over, it is often the primitive dances, the movement, that is lost first.

In the 19th century in Europe the tradition of pantomimes with stock characters (the clown, Harlequin, Pierrot, Columbine) was still very much alive. With the advent of the cinema, many of these stock characters were transferred and given new life in the silent movies by such great mime artists as Buster Keaton and Charlie Chaplin. Then came sound and more and more machines to take over the work of the body, and gradually America sat down! We have become a very passive society, scarcely using our legs to walk to the corner store, let alone for any creative concern. We spend our days sitting in cars and buses and chairs, in front of big meals, and television sets, typewriters, and tables.

We have even tried to brainwash people from ethnic backgrounds where the body is traditionally used to help expression (Italian, Spanish, Black, Jewish, etc.) "Don't talk with your hands!" we tell public speaking students, in deference, I guess, to a WASP tradition of the stiff upper lip, and even stiffer body to accompany it.

Yet sociologists tell us that the reign of the WASP is on the wane in our society. The day is coming when more and more of our leaders will come from ethnic groups who subscribe to a less formal life style. We are educating these future leaders now. What better way than mime to teach the best and most natural forms of communication through the body?

Pantomime is Suitable For All Children

It is true that in sport and physical education, the child or adult has some outlet for body movement, but for many who are not "good at games," the competition is hard to take, and leaves very little to the imagination. For these children, not sports minded or gymnastically inclined, mime is a great outlet for body energy.

Then there are children with language barriers. I have taught Spanish-speaking and Indian children who were expected to be fluent in two languages. What a relief it was, for these children, to come to the silent art, where there is no need for "words, words, words."

It is also true that, when a person is free physically, he will be led, naturally and easily, to vocal freedom.

It is not surprising, either, that pantomime is an art form where less-bright children sometimes excel intelligent children, whose physical response is often slower. On many occasions I have approached a group of children labeled "dull," "slow," "E.S.N," and found them to be the most creative, the most free, much to the amazement of their teachers. What a thrill for these children to be the best at something, when they have become accustomed to being at the bottom of the achievement ladder. I am not saying that bright children cannot do just as well in pantomime, but often their movement is less spontaneous, because they are so used to using their brains, and pantomime comes best from the heart. It is, someone has said, "the language of the heart expressed through the language of the body."

The place to start this creative training of the body is the elementary school. We cannot imagine an elementary school today where paints and crayons, gym mats and rhythm band instruments are not available to the children, yet we are neglecting to use the best instrument our children have: their bodies.

Creative Drama and Mime

You may already be using creative drama in your classroom. For some time now, in schools across the country, creative drama has been recognized

. as an art form in itself, particularly suited to children;

. and an exciting and creative way of teaching other subjects in the curriculum, breathing a little life and energy into the world of purple mimeographed papers and texts.

Mime has been, for the most part, considered on the side lines. Many of the books on drama have a chapter on pantomime as a useful and fun technique that will lead into the world of improvisation or the scripted play.

I would like to consider mime, however, as a world unto itself. . .an art form that is equally suited to the children's needs. . .an art form to be enjoyed for its own sake. I would like to see Mime lessons allotted time on the time table, just like Art, Music, Creative Drama, or Poetry. In the chapters that follow you will find different areas of mime — warm-ups to begin with, occupational work, and exploration of animals, characters, objects and feelings. Section II gives many exciting ways to extend mime through masks, and Section III contains scenarios of mime plays that can be used as culminating activities. From these you could draw a year's curriculum, teaching mime once a week.

Who Teaches Mime?

On most occasions, I have come to a school as a specialist teacher. This has disadvantages. It means that I have to spend a certain amount of time finding out what the children know. For many exercises, I am presuming a preparation period or a study unit. If I had worked in the school all week, I would know when dinosaurs, or American Indians, were the order of the day. On the other hand, it's nice for someone with specialized training to come in as a "new" person to teach a subject that's considered a treat.

If you do not have a drama specialist in your school system, another likely candidate, in many schools, is the Physical Education teacher. Particularly in the Elementary school, where the emphasis is not so heavily into competitive sports, many P.E. teachers are already incorporating mime and modern dance techniques into their classes.

But there may be no mime specialist in your school. Many a classroom teacher finds— to her delight — that she too can teach mime. Even if you are burdened with a whole curriculum to teach, and cannot see a special time set aside for mime, look into Chapter VII for integrating mime into other subject areas.

The Role of The Teacher

Many teachers feel hesitant to start pantomime because they feel uncomfortable doing it themselves. Kenneth Tynan called pantomime "The gentle art of frigging about in tights". . .and many teachers just do not see themselves in that image! Fear not, it is not absolutely necessary for you yourself to take part. You do not want the children to imitate you, as you might if you were a dance teacher demonstrating a particular step, or technique. Rather, you are there to give the inspiration for the child to create for himself. When teaching pantomime myself, I very rarely join in, except perhaps in an opening session. I am much too interested in watching the progress of the class. I hate the thought that a child may be creating something unique, catch sight of what I am doing, and stop his movement to copy mine.

If you do not have to be a mime artist supreme, what then is needed? First, and most important, the belief that every child in your class *can* respond in some way. Eventually even the lazy, fat child, who hates to pretend, who hates to exert herself at all may someday *do* something. I can say without equivocation that all children, as part of their human heritage, can move expressively, if given the chance.

Second, a belief in your own creativity, and the powers of your own imagination After all, if you are teaching children, you have chosen "people watching" as part of your profession, so you may as well explore the whole person.

Third, a sense of rhythm. Pantomime is an art form, and it seems to me that perhaps the one feature that all art has in common is rhythm. Dance, music (from every part of the world), painting, sculpture, good theatre, poetry, all respond to a beat. . .an inner dynamism. A good pantomime class establishes a rhythm of creativity between teacher and children that is almost as tangible as the rhythm in this frieze from ancient Greece. If the voice on the intercom interrupts, or the janitor enters, everyone in the mime class will respond to this break in rhythm.

If you have already worked with the body through physical education or dance, or you have already experimented with pantomime as an introduction to creative drama or a rehearsal technique in working on a play. . .if you are an art teacher who would like to carry the use of form and color into movement. . .if you are teaching everything from math to music and you are tired of writing on the board and handing out those "purple ditto papers" — then try and see yourself working with the ideas in the next twenty chapters. To teach, and to perform any kind of pantomime requires a constantly moving film-strip of the imagination, unwinding inside your head. *All* the children I have worked with have had this capacity to imagine. It is the mime teacher's job to respond to these colorful and vital images, providing a stimulus, a framework, for the body to turn that "filmstrip" into dynamic movement.

There is one other important reason for using pantomime with children. They love it! I once taught pantomime in an elementary school on a weekly basis. I had to fetch the children from their home room to take them down to the gym. When my head appeared above the glass in the doorway, the whole class cheered! (And I should add, before taking any bouquets for popularity, that it was Pantomime that earned the applause, not I, because I've taught many other subjects without getting that response!)

The teaching of pantomime (or mime, as I will call it for convenience from now on) requires a great deal of mental preparation. Each lesson should follow a logical sequence, and build on a solid structure of ideas, feeding from the children. Ideas for a mime lesson occur to me at the strangest times, and are developed in my head while I'm doing a mindless chore like loading the dishwasher or stuck in a traffic jam. It is a good idea to make a practice of jotting down ideas as they come to you, and then finding a place for them in your schedule.

Does this all sound rather business-like and uncreative? Business-like, yes——because mime is a disciplined art form——but uncreative, no. Creativity should not be an excuse for chaos, and children do not enjoy themselves. . .do not create. . .in a totally permissive atmosphere. To say "Let's all be animals," "Now let's put out a fire," "Now, we're all going to be beach balls," or "Could you all be monsters?" is just asking for trouble. You'll have monsters all right!

If you come well-prepared—— but flexible enough to respond to the mood of the moment, the children will never ask, "Why are we doing this?" And even if they do, you'll have the answer.

From the very first lesson it is essential to lay down the "rules of the game": no sound, unless I ask for it, and everyone participates. Do not allow casual audience members, particularly during the first few classes, when you are trying to build confidence and concentration. If a child refuses to join in, allow him to watch for a certain period of time, and then ask him to join in a group activity where another person is needed. If he still refuses (unless there are extenuating circumstances of a psychological nature) send him away.

Children often copy one another at the beginning— — which means the private film strip is not working in their heads— — so you have to try a very concentrated exercise— — and constantly remind them to "do their own thing."

Where To Begin?

In a large room, preferably— — but out of doors is also very possible, even desirable, for some types of mime. The beginnings of western theatre are with the Greeks, and all their drama was performed in the open air. A natural setting is often provided by trees, hills, rocks and bushes, so mime is a great subject for summer camps or recreation programs.

Indoors, an empty, large room is best of all (a gym or all-purpose room), but if you cannot afford that luxury you will have to push back the desks and use the classroom. One advantage to desks is that they do create different levels. Much of the mime described in this book has worked much better because I was able to use a variety of different levels— — hiding places, shelters and ramps. How much more effective to mime a monkey up in a tree if you can use another level for the tree. Mask work depends greatly on surprise techniques. Without a door, a screen or a curtain, it is hard to make an interesting entrance. Do not throw away the old scenery from the sixth grade musical; it may come in handy for your mime classes. In a school, the stage— — used "in the round"— — may prove your best available space. This is also true of many church or temple facilities.

Ideally, I would want a studio-type room (no mirror— — mime is not ballet) with moveable platforms and risers to create ramps, steps, and some interesting shapes with holes— — the kind of modern sculpture that children like to play in. I have seen some modern sculpture pieces in the courtyards of museums that I have coveted for my mime classes.

Since I do not think that classic mime in a totally bare environment, accompanied only by silence, is the right kind of experience for children, I'd also include one or two tables and chairs or stools in my ideal mime studio. Some lighting effects, with basic red, gold, green and blue gelatins on a dimmer system would also be useful. A tape recorder, a record player and some percussion instruments (cymbal, drum, triangle, bells, wood blocks) and a box of junk "props"— — a baton, a crown, a broom, a spoon, some wooden swords and knives, some cloths) would be wonderful on a permanent basis. I always drag all my junk with me in the trunk of my car. My ideal studio would have many shelves at different levels around the walls for the different masks and paraphernalia.

What To Wear?

Leotards and footless tights are the most appropriate dress for mime, but I have never found boys who liked to wear tights. Plain long pants with turtle-neck sweaters are equally good. I prefer bare feet— —because feet can say as much as hands. Blue jeans and or striped sweat shirt with long sleeves are also fine, even if you feel less "professional." Always carry a spare pair of shorts and T-shirt, in case a child comes dressed in something totally unsuitable like a party dress.

If you are going to participate, then you will want to spread the group out all over the room, and move in circles. In case you would rather dictate and watch, you will need a look-out post, preferably on another level from the rest of the group. The group will focus most of its work in your direction.

Starting The Creative Juices Running

To begin, you must warm up your body and your mind. The difference between limbering for a sport and limbering for mime is that you are setting your mind thinking in all kinds of creative ways. I can almost name the moment when the group I am working with is relaxed, concentrating and alive. Sometimes it never happens — — and that is a bad class.

Most children are naturally relaxed — — at least physically — — but they need some kind of experience which will take them away from the "real" world and into the world of the imagination, an experience which also says, "Look what my body can say!" Here are twenty good warm-up exercises, useful for all age groups. Your favorites may be repeated at the beginning of any lesson. An older, more experienced class should be in the habit of warming up by themselves when they first come into the room.
All these exercises are done by everyone together, so there should be no feeling of inhibition if everyone is busy working and concentrating. In most cases you will need a "freeze" signal — — a drum, a cymbal, or a tamborine. Otherwise you need a group that is well trained to listen to your voice.

1. *Wake up!*
   "You are curled up asleep on the floor. When you hear this sound: ("Wake up!" — — or cymbal) stretch and yawn with your whole body. Yawn with your mouth, your tummy, your elbows. . .with your back, with your knees. . .but you will *not* get up! Go back to sleep. This time, just stretch one arm. . .let it flop down. . .now the other, and let *it* flop down. Now one leg. . .flop down. . . now the other leg. . .flop down. . .now your behind. . .your back. . .your head. I think you are ready to get up. You can then check each part of the body, standing up. Wake up, hands! (Shake them). Arms (Shake them). . .head. . . hips. . .legs. . .tongue. You are wonderfully awake. You're moving all over like a dancing jellyfish (use tamborine). . .and relax."

2. *Golden Apples*

   "They are hanging from the ceiling just beyond your reach. Each one is worth a thousand dollars. Try and reach them with one hand. . .the other hand. . . both hands. No good. Try jumping for them. All to no avail. Golden apples have moved beyond that barbed wire fence over there (point right about two feet off floor). Stretch yourself out horizontally. . .one way. . .now the other. No good. Try lying on the floor and stretching out. Perhaps you can reach them that way. Yes, I think you have one. . .two. . .three! Throw them up in the air. Juggle with them. Sit down. Eat an apple. Just as you are on your last bite, you turn into gold yourself. Shine!! (Tamborine!!)"

3. *Elastic People*

   (Here you will need to delve into your junk box for several long pieces of elastic — about 3 yards long. Take one for every two children — — i.e., for a class of 20 you need 10 elastics, each joined at the end to form a circle.)

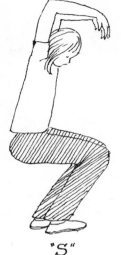

"S"

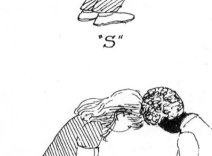

"A"

The children face one another each holding the elastic, or wearing it around their waists. On cue from you, they stretch and snap, making as interesting shapes as possible. Now move like robots, still with the elastics. Freeze. Now you are crazy marionettes and you cannot get out of these rubber bands.

(This lesson can also be done *without* the elastics. The children are the rubber bands, stretching in all different directions, starting floppy and small and then stretching out.)

4. *Alphabets*

(This warm-up exercise is expandable to 26 lessons. . .A to Z. . .or else you can just mix up the letters and use it when you wish. Marcel Marceau has a beautiful Alphabet Mime book, with a picture of a still-life for each letter of the alphabet. This was my inspiration for this idea.)

"Starting with the letter A——draw it very large in the air. With your finger. . . your elbow. . .your foot. . .your tongue. Now try a lower-case a. Now see if you can make yourself into a capital A." Maybe two or three children will get together like the alphabet dancers on Sesame Street.

Now I ask for some words that begin with A——perhaps apple. . .angry. . . airplane. . .afraid. . .axe. . .America. I jot them down as they give them to me. I then call out the first word, "apple" and ask the children for their response, in movement, to this word. With my drum they freeze into a still-life (like Marcel Marceau). I then go into my next word: "angry," and so on.

5. *Cartoon Characters*

The action in all cartoons, is fast, furious, and fantastical. With partners, choose two favorite cartoon characters (e.g. Tom and Jerry). Discuss things that happen in cartoons. . .shinning down ropes, falling off cliffs, hiding, chasing about, flying, shooting out of a cannon. Play some fast music (tape it from any television cartoon) and act out the movie.

6. *Villages*

Set up four "houses" in the four corners of the room, with four different musical instruments —— perhaps tamborine in one corner, drum in another, woodblocks in the third and maracas in the last. Assign children to different houses. In a class of twenty, five to each house. Play each instrument, and ask the children, "Who lives in that house?" The rhythm you choose for each instrument will greatly affect the answers you receive. You might hear of in-habitants such as

. The Whirligigs, who cannot stop whirling around (Maracas)
. The Galloping Giants (Woodblocks)
. The ippety-skippety elves (Tamborine)
. The mad, one-legged monsters. (They hop) (Drum)

When the children hear their rhythm and their instrument, they come from their houses to the center of the room (galloping, whirling, skipping, hopping); then return home. Next, they can change houses (On signal, "All change!") until everyone has had a turn in each house.

"N"

7. *Bridges*

Make bridge shapes with your body –– any way you choose –– strong bridges, twisted old bridges, fat bridges, delicate "I am scared to go across" bridges.

Divide the class into two groups. One group are the bridges; the other the travellers. They must go under, over, through the bridges. Now reverse: The travellers are the bridges. Do it again. This time the travellers are blind (with eyes closed).

End the whole exercise with one vast bridge made by the whole group. Remember, bridges can open up to allow boats to go through, and many different vehicles travel on bridges: motorcycles, trucks, cars, bicycles, trailers, buses.

8. *Magic Magnets*

From your junk box, take out as many colored squares of paper (approximately 12" x 12") as there are children in your group. Give each child a square, and tell them to put it somewhere on the floor that is "home" for them. Stand on magic square. It has magnetic power and will always pull you back "home." A strong wind is blowing you off your magic magnet, but by a count of twelve you must be home. Now try sneaking away on tip-toe from your magic magnet. The clock strikes twelve again and, like Cinderella, you must return home. Try crawling away on the floor, on your stomach. You get so far, at the count of six, but then the magic magnet starts to pull you back home again, by twelve. Now try creeping away on hands and knees in a circle No use –– by twelve, you are dizzy, but you are home.

9. *Rag Dolls* (Good for Kindergarteners)

Ask the children to bring in their floppiest doll, and show us just how floppy the real doll can be. Put the dolls in some place where they can watch the children (here is where your shelves can be so useful). "Now copy your own doll. Show her that your head. . .your arms. . .your hands. . .your back. . . your legs. . .your feet. . .are just as floppy as hers." Have a floppy doll parade around the room. (Will they all make it without flopping over?) Use some floppy music or maracas or tamborine.

10. *Wind-up Toys*

Ask the children to bring in a wind-up or mechanical toy (clockwork mice, soldiers, walking dolls, trains, barking dogs and so forth). Choose some of the toys and, using some kind of mechanical wind-up noise (the toy, or I just make it up myself) — — all act out a variety of mechanical toys, and move at the same time as the toy. When the toy runs out — — and stops — — so do the children.

11. *Puzzles*

Start with children in a circle. On a signal one child runs to the center of the circle and makes her body into a piece of puzzle. Next child fits into that puzzle piece with his own shape — — and so on until you have a giant-size puzzle. This can be done flat on the floor — — like a jigsaw — — or upright.

A good variation is *Moving Puzzles*. Move any way you wish to music (Either recorded music or use a drum). When the music stops, freeze. Look around and see whose shape your shape will fit into. Move, holding the shape. Then freeze in clusters, until the music starts again.

12. *Little and Big*

On a signal from you, the children grow from very large to small, and vice versa. "Curl up very tiny because you are an

. acorn. . .magically grown to an oak tree!
. match-box car shooting around. . .suddenly become a full-size car.
. a mouse. . .turning into an elephant.
. a fly. . .turning into an airplane
. a tricycle. . .now a garbage truck
. cottonballs. . .turn into thunder clouds
. a tiny, very bouncy ball. . .growing into a huge beach ball.

13. *Magic Glasses*

(I use the plastic straps from a 6-pack container of soda or beer, and cut the straps into 3 pairs of magic glasses. You need one pair per child.)

"Curl up asleep in your bed. You have a wonderful dream. You are the owner of Magic Glasses. Wake up. . .stretch. . .find the Magic Glasses and put them on. Look all around you, high and low, far and wide. What do you see?"

I ask the children for suggestions and choose a few adventures with Magic Glasses. . .e.g., everything is made of candy.

14. *Bubble Gum*

In a circle, as the tamborine shakes, each child runs into the center of the circle and stops when the tamborine stops. They must stick to one another like bubble gum.

"Roll up very small and round like a gum ball in a bubble-gum machine. A little girl comes along and first, she shakes the machine. (She shakes you, too). Then she drops a penny in, you roll down and out into the little girl's hand. She carries you along, then she opens two fingers, you roll out, and someone comes along and steps on you, squashing you flat."

"This time, the little girl carries you very carefully in her hand and gives you to her father. He puts you in his mouth and chews and chews. Then he pushes his tongue against you, and blows you into a big bubble. Then he chews you all up again, and blows another bubble. This time he pinches you at the corner and you become a floating bubble-gum balloon. You float around until slowly the air is leaving you, and you are just a flat, chewed-up piece of gum, stuck on the floor, in any shape you wish."

15. *Clay*

Everyone knows clay — — how heavy it is — — how it feels. "Imagine you are a big lump of clay. Someone just dropped you on the floor. To a drum beat (big and heavy) move just a little — — along the floor — — Now move up into the air. Now very slowly, just like clay, move towards another piece of clay, and get stuck. Break away! Get stuck again in another place — — like two heavy-weight boxers! Come apart. Mould yourself into something

. plain and smooth
. very fancy
. flat and squashed

. round and roly-poly
. wiggly
. spiky

Now take partners. One of you is the lump of clay, the other one the sculptor Make an animal or bird statue. . .something silly. . .something serious and sad. . .anything you choose. Change over: the one who was the clay now has a turn to be the sculptor.

16. *Ribbons*

From your junk-box take out some long silky (preferably scarlet) ribbon. Show the children how the ribbon moves. You can drop it on the floor in a heap. . . you can trail it along. . .you can make it zig-zag or dance. . .you can let it blow back and forth. Any way you move them, ribbons are soft, free-flowing. Put on the song "Scarlet Ribbons." Now the children are the ribbons, blowing in the breeze, trailing on the floor, even tied up in a beautiful bow.

17. *Wire*

This time take a long piece of wire from your junk box. Whichever way you bend it, wire stays where you put it, so you can make many different shapes. What else is wire used for? To join things together, to hang things from, to support things. (The child should give you some good answers here.) To a staccato drumbeat, they now become the wire. First a long, straight piece — then bent slightly, now with a little hook for the top, now bent in half, now in a circle. . .and so forth.

18. *"I am Deaf"*

"I cannot hear words," I tell the children "but there are certain things I would like to know. I want you to show me, in movement"

. An Ocean. (Children will show, in their movements, "Big". . ."It has waves". . ."Wet". . ."Ships sail in it". . ."Fish swim in it", etc.)

. A City. (Traffic going honk——honk. . .big high buildings. . .lots of people all rushing about. . .delivery men, builders, mailmen, etc.

. Swings. (Go back and forth; pump; sometimes you can go very high, sometimes slowly on a hot day. Sometimes a friend pushes you. You can even stand on a swing.)

Use any word you, the deaf person, would like to have explained to you in mime.

19. *Statues*

"Shake all over, like jello, to the sound of the tamborine. When the music stops, show me some different statues: happy. . .angry. . .scared. . .fat. . . silly. . .dizzy. . .sad. . .sneezing. . .bored." (This is an excellent warm-up exercise to lead into work on feelings.)

20. *Trips*

"If you were not here, in this place, right now, where would you like to be? Up in a tree? On a trampoline? On a beach? Skiing? Sky-diving? In a hammock? Driving through the city?" Children will all take a trip to the place of their choice. When I give the signal, everyone freezes —— I ask a few questions —— and we all take a trip to the most appealing places.

"Now make yourself very, very small. We are going to take another trip. . . but this time you are an ant. Work your way through straight hair. . .now long and silky hair, now short and curly hair. . .across the skin. . .through a wool sweater, up and over the buttons and down the other side until you reach a brick wall. Climb all the way down the wall till you reach your anthill. What a trip!

All these exercises are good beginnings, to get the children moving. Teachers often say they like mime because "you're not supposed to talk;" it helps with discipline. I find that once children understand the rules of the game: —— "No talking" —— discipline is rarely a problem in mime. In Creative Drama, a class can easily get out of control when everyone is improvising dialogue, and all talking at once. In Mime, the child is too busy concentrating, making that "film strip in the head" come alive. The importance of the warm-up session cannot be stressed enough. It does not even need to be a physical warm-up. On a day when everyone tumbles into the room, shrieking and wild, you may want to start with something quiet and concentrated like *Ribbons* (16), spending a good deal of time demonstrating the flow and form of the colorful ribbons. Or you may want to capitalize on all this terrific energy, and put them all in monster masks —— or go straight into a warm-up like *Bubble Gum* (14).

A warm-up session may take 5 minutes or 50. It can develop into a whole lesson. *Bridges* (7) has taken up a whole period on more than one occasion, when the children wanted to experiment with many different kinds of vehicles and ships passing over and under the bridge. One day we even had a July 4 Parade march over the bridge!

As you develop free expressive movements in your warm-ups, you will become aware that in the course of a lesson, the children are handling many different imaginary objects. In fact, occupational mime is the most familiar form of mime, and even very small children can be aware of imaginary doors, cakes, windows, flowers — — whatever we use.

I feel that occupational mime work is most useful in the older grades. I do not think it matters very much if a 5-year-old is blithely banging her fist on the floor, "hammering," but a 10-year-old should acquire some technique, should progress beyond the feel of the movement involved in hammering to some knowledge of the weight, shape, and size of the hammer she is using. Left to their own devices, most children will improvise very hurriedly — — often carelessly — — so that quite often an improvised scene will last only a few minutes — — even if the story line is very involved. I am often amazed to hear the children tell a long complicated story after a few moments of hasty excited improvisation.

Assume right from the beginning that if a thing is worth doing, it is worth doing properly. Concentration is most important in occupational mime. . .and very clear large movements. In mime, every gesture should tell us something new!

Finding the Essential Details

Here is a picture a 4-year-old drew of her music teacher in her music room. You will notice that she only included the elements that really mattered to her — — no chairs, no windows, no tables — — just the essentials for music making.

In a way, children are like impressionists in their art work. So it is with mime. Only the important movements are needed. We give an *illusion* of an action which in reality would be much busier, and perhaps take longer. The impressionist did not paint every minute detail in a bunch of flowers, nor would the good mime artist use every little movement involved in picking that bunch of flowers.

With the movements that you do choose to represent, the main objective in occupational mime is truth of action. Children understand this very well. Watching a mime show, or watching one another, they will scrutinize the action like the most demanding critics. "He walked through the wall!" "She forgot the box was supposed to be very heavy." "That's not the way you hold a scissors." They expect to be told the truth in movement as much as they do in words.

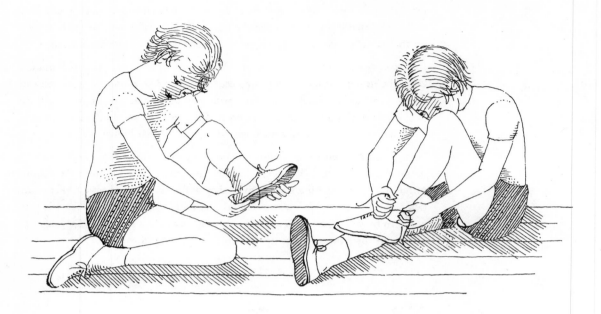

A Good Way to Introduce Occupational Mime

It is a good idea to start with real objects. I like the old game of blind-folding a child and then letting him/her pick an object from a sack or bag and, through touch alone, guess what the object is. Emphasize such aspects as weight. . .size . . .texture, so the children become familiar with these terms. Then let them do one simple action, such as taking off a shoe and putting it on again. Then, remembering all the movements, repeat the action in mime.

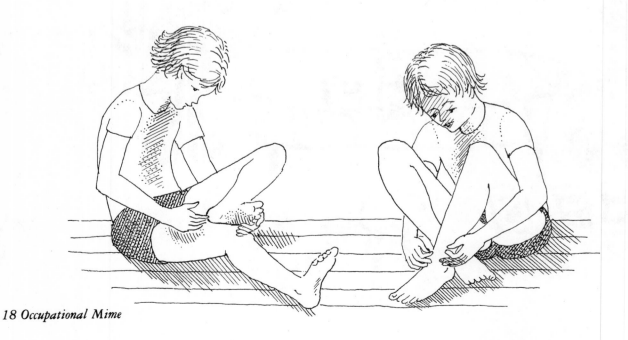

"Passing the Object"

Here's an exercise that can be done at all grade levels with equally good results; kindergarteners are often just as good as fifth graders. Seat the children in a circle or several small circles (here is where your student teacher or teacher's aide would be invaluable.) Starting with one child, pass around different objects. Get the child to pick up a large empty imaginary box and put it in the center of the circle. This is for holding all the objects. You might pass around — —

. a stack of dishes
. a poisonous snake
. a prickly porcupine
. old-fashioned, very sticky fly-paper
. a diamond ring
. an ice cube
. a fluffy chick
. a basket of eggs
. a snowball
. a slinky
. a dirty rag

You can add to the list, and have some fun trying to move the box after it's been filled with that strange assortment of objects.

With older grades, the children enjoy watching each other. Divide the group in two, and let one group watch the other and suggest objects to be passed around. Change groups after a while so all the children get a turn to watch. I find them very critical of one another.

The first child to pick up an object establishes its size, weight, and texture, so I number the children, or call out different names, to give everyone a turn to begin the action. If scenes develop within the group, make sure they keep their concentration and the truth of the mime. Of course they should not talk. If, for example, John puts the diamond ring in his pocket, the rest of the group must react in mime. Often other objects will join the original one. A magnifying glass may be brought out to examine the diamond ring, and the next child will want to use it.

There are many variations to the handling of simple objects. A game I have played with great success in mime is the changing ball game. In creative dramatics, I let speech develop, but the game is more fun, more successful, if done entirely in mime. I put the children into circles of 5 or 6 children, using all the space available. Toss an imaginary basketball among the group. If you have a drum or cymbal, you can regulate the throws with a definite signal each time the ball is thrown. The children should "know" the ball — — the size and weight in particular — — and it must remain the same until, on your established signal (either "Stop!" or a whistle or a cymbal clash) everyone freezes, and the ball changes. You might make it — —

20 times heavier
100 times heavier
Covered with prickles
Glass
Hot
Slippery

Furry
Extra bouncy
Very light

The ball can get bigger — — so big it takes up the whole circle. On signal it disappears to almost nothing. It can gradually get smaller and smaller, or else suddenly shrink to a pin head.

Developing concentration

I find the concentration of older grades can be captured if, after all this excitement, you describe one of the balls in minute detail.

Let's take the ball when it becomes glass. Have the children sit down, in their circles or at their desks. Each child picks up his/her own glass ball. I usually let the children decide on a color, and I do not specify size, except that throughout the rest of the lesson I remind them that the ball stays the same.

Here's the kind of minute observation that grades 4, 5, and 6 will especially enjoy:

> You have just picked up your glass ball. Let's take a good look at it. Let's get to know it, so that is almost seems real to you. I'm going to ask you some questions about your glass ball. Don't tell me the answers; tell yourself, silently. Hold the ball in one hand — — now in the other. How heavy is it? Now hold it in both hands. Is is smooth glass, or are there rough spots? Hold the glass ball up to the light. Have you ever looked into something made of glass and seen other things reflected in the light?

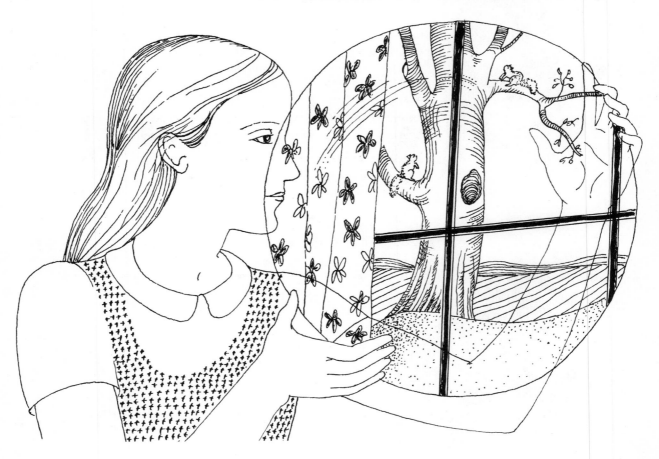

Let's imagine there's a window with curtains — — red curtains and a mobile
hanging in the window. Can you see that in your glass ball? If you turn
it one way, the window looks a funny shape. Through the window there's
a big tree — — a mulberry tree — — and the squirrels are having a good
time scampering along the branches to eat the mulberries. Turn your glass
ball a bit — — oh, there goes a squirrel! Put your glass ball down on the
floor (or on your desk). Remember it still feels the same and it's still just
as heavy.

An extraordinary exploration of the powers of the imagination can take place here.
Not only are the children imagining a glass ball that is not there. . .they also see
something else, reflected in that imaginary picture; through that, they see yet
another image. From the private imaginary "camera in the head" to the ball. . .
to the window. . .to the tree. . .to the squirrel. . .layer upon layer. Yet the thinking process is logical, methodical. For occupational mime, this is a necessity. Behind every precise manipulation of any object in mime, there must be a very clear
thought.

Sometimes I play a trick on the children and, accidently-on-purpose, tread on someone's glass ball. If the child is angry with me, I'm very pleased — — it means he was
really using his imagination. One class asked, "Can we take our glass balls to the
lunch room?" I said, "Fine, as long as you don't forget and leave them there."
The lunch ladies told me the children kept their imaginary glass balls all through
lunch. One boy even took his home with him. His mother complained that he
took it everywhere he went — — even to bed!

I happen to have a green glass ball, used in lobster fishing, and I brought it to
class the day after we had done the exercises with the imaginary glass ball. The
comments were most interesting:"My ball was much bigger/heavier/nicer/smoother/
prettier/smaller than that." We then developed a mime scene, based on lobster fishing, and developed a great deal of good occupational mime cooperatively — — handling nets and wet ropes, pulling in boats and holding lobster. You might turn
your glass ball into a crystal ball, and develop all kinds of scenes in a Fortune
Teller's tent.

Achieving Concentration with Younger Children

I use a simple story, like the Shoemaker and the Elves. While the shoemaker is
asleep, all the children (as elves) take leather and a pair of scissors, and cut out
the shapes of two little shoes.

Again, I would ask questions about the "truthfulness" of the leather (What color? How thick? Is it difficult to cut? Are your scissors sharp enough?) Then we stitch. Most children, sewing in mime, will sew in a continuous circle, forgetting that after putting the needle into the leather, they must then take their fingers away, in order to pull the needle through.

Having sewn the shoes, the children may pick a fancy lace, and lace up the shoes, even tying an imaginary bow (Kindergartners are probably learning to do this with real bows). Then let the children thoroughly examine the shoes they have made and then tiptoe to the front of the room and put the shoes beside the sleeping shoe-maker. I have used a teachers' aide as the shoemaker. On a signal, he/she wakes up and is delighted to find the shoes and admire the craftsmanship. Again, the children will call out such things as, "You haven't looked at mine! The red pair, with soft leather and blue laces!"

So far, we have considered the manipulation of objects, with the hands alone. Yet if we look at the every-day world of occupation, many jobs are done using other parts of the body. A good warm-up exercise for occupational work is to give the children a great variety of jobs, using many different parts of the body. Use a signal, such as a whistle, or the "freeze" technique as you change jobs.

. Pull a big heavy rope with a boat full of fish all the way up to the shore.
. Swing a heavy axe to chop down a tree.
. Start a gas lawn-mower, or have difficulties with a different kind of mower.
. Look through a giant telescope at the stars.
. Use an old-fashioned treadle sewing machine.
. Paint a ceiling.
. Dig a garden in hot sun.
. Row a boat.
. Tread grapes for making grape juice.
. Pick strawberries.
. Jump on a trampoline.
. Scrub a dirty floor.
. Ring a heavy bell.
. Look through several key holes, till you find what you are looking for.
. Wash a car.
. Arrange flowers in a vase.
. Count money.
. Put up a tent.
. Go underwater to examine a sunken ship.
. Build a sand castle.
. Take pictures, close up and far away.

Most children tend to think of their hands as their only instrument of expression. In the above exercises you, the teacher, should be aware of interesting *backs*, agile *feet*, the angle of the *elbows*. It is obviously good to have some space to move around, and each child will need his or her own private area of creativity in which there is room to move.

Once they know what the actual job is, the children are ready to move on to the thought of *who* is working. Children of all ages are usually interested in the idea that a job may be different, if done by someone else. My brother was sitting in the dining room and heard me working in the kitchen. He did not know whether it was me or my mother but, as he listened to the rhythm of the banging cupboard doors, the clatter of the pots and pans, he decided it must be me. I work in a more slapdash way than my methodical mother.

The teacher can set up a definite real job (not an imaginary pantomime), such as cleaning the blackboard or clearing a table, and then ask three or four children in the class to do the job in their own way. Some will be brisk and purposeful in their movements, others careless, some slow and exact. Everyone moves differently!

Now any of the jobs suggested above can be repeated, thinking of two things:

1. The reality of the job,
2. Who is performing the job.

For example, the old-fashioned treadle sewing machine may be used by

. A very old, short-sighted tailor;
. A child who has been told not to touch it;
. A busy mother making clothes for her children.

You may look through the keyhole as

. A spy on a dangerous foreign assignment.
. A little old lady;
. A child, locked out of the house.

You may count money as

. A pompous bank manager, with big cigar;
. A blind beggar in a poor country;
. A robber who has just stolen the money;
. A four-year-old emptying a bank.

Or paint a picture as

. The world's most modern artist;
. A very careful old person who is copying a photograph;
. A teenager, very bored in an art class.

So far we have established two important elements in occupational mime: *what* is being done, and *who* is doing it. I think older children can appreciate one more element, already hinted at — emotion. Many mechanical jobs can be made quite different to look at by adding feelings. If I scrub the floor as a fat old cleaning lady who is feeling very happy because she just won $1,000, I would scrub it very differently from the fat old lady who just *lost* $1,000.

Older children should be made aware that in mime, it is easier to find one element at a time. (In fact, this applies to acting in general.) *First,* concentrate on the scrubbing itself; how to hold the mop; where he pail is; and how full of water. *Second,* add the character of the fat lady. *Third,* add the age, and *fourth,* think of that $1,000 and feel happy!

Of course it can work from the inside out, starting with the feelings, and then adding the various characteristics. But one of this should be done unless the actual pantomime itself — the job, the scrubbing — is done well.

Occupational pantomime could easily last for a whole semester, or several weeks, and culminate in a group project involving everyone, such as

A pirate ship. Start from early morning when everyone is asleep, except the captain, and go about the business of the day until. . .What adventure could they have on this particular day?

The auto-body shop. Business is slack, until someone brings in a very wrecked car.

A diner. Go from breakfast, for working people, very busy, to lunch, for people out shopping, on a lunch break, and dinner, with everyone tired at the end of a long day, waiting for the new shift.

An airplane. Pilot, stewards and stewardesses, and passengers, going about their business until an engine goes dead.

Firemen, putting out a fire.

To all these occupations you can add your own colorful characters and various feelings. Do not forget that the weather, the time of day, and the environment will all add to the scene.

Making Occupational Mime Dramatic

It's very interesting to visit a factory, a post office, a library, a town hall, and then come back and mime your own work place. . .especially if something out of the ordinary should occur in the course of the regular routine. This gives each scene a sense of structure, of building a climax. In real life, much occupational work feels as if it has no structure — and for many children. . .and adults. . .a job is just an endless chore. If the occupational mime scene is to be something more than acting out activity, then it should have an element of surprise, a sense of rhythm that will make it dramatic. I have tried to suggest this in the group projects. It is worth looking for one good, single, exciting happening in the midst of the routine. You do not have to look yourself; you can set up a mime scene in the gift-wrapping department of a large store at Christmas time, or the construction site of a new house, and the children will certainly have ideas for. . .what could happen if —?

"I am 12. I have to play an old lady of 84. How should I move?"

"I really want to play Peter Pan. Everyone says I look right and I speak right, but I'm such a Klutz. I want to be light and nimble."

"I'm supposed to play this wicked murderer. I've never murdered anyone. How do I know what it feels like?"

"I've got to play the boy's part and I hate it. I'm a girl. I just wish I knew what to do."

One aspect of mime work that teachers sometimes overlook is how useful it can be in preparing characterization in a play. It is difficult enough for an adult actor to assume another character, and yet teachers will often expect children to do this, without any help. I remember visiting an elementary school where two teachers were putting on a big musical production. Two more frustrated people I have yet to meet! The cause of their aggravation? The children refused to act their characters. They just stood on the stage, and recited their lines in a stilted fashion. The teachers could not understand why. They had chosen the cast from their very best readers, and the songs were fine.

Everybody knew their lines. But the show was "dead."

The answer was that they had put the cart before the horse. The children had memorized their lines before they knew their characters or thought about movement. I spent a session with the cast in mime and movement, incorporating many of the character walks and occupations of the play itself. We also added more blocking (movement) to the lines, and added some unusual entrances and exits, using the whole auditorium, not just the right and left of the small platform stage. When the play was repeated at the next rehearsal, things had livened up considerably. We had breathed a little life into the characters.

While it is certainly true that all children are natural mimics, many appear to lose this ability as they grow older. Five-year-olds do not discriminate over who will be best to play the role of mother or father when they are playing house. They know all the kids in the neighborhood can do it. But as children learn to read and write, they become more self-conscious about "throwing themselves" wholeheartedly into a role — unless we are talking about the children in the class we call "hams."

Character mime can help overcome the older child's inhibitions, and help him "find the character" — a task acting schools all over the world spend years in doing! And even when you aren't working on a play, character mime is an important way of finding out about other people — and yourself.

Starting From the Outside-In

For children, I believe the easiest way is to start from the outside. This is the way most children see people anyway. They are very quick to judge by externals. . .how people look. They are also very much aware of how people move, from television movies. So I begin my character work with a *Famous People Parade.* The children parade around the room, stopping at a strategic point for me to guess who they are: George Washington, Archie Bunker, Bugs Bunny, Fred Flintstone, Lucille Ball, Cher, the President. . .

The one great obvious character difference lies in the sexes. Do you want all the class — boys and girls — to act cute and coy and feminine, or take on the role of the macho tough guy? My own thought about this is that everyone acts everything. Let me hastily add that I realize that at a certain age boys and girls will scarcely touch one another, let alone act out a character of the opposite sex. But if you are firm: "Everyone does everything," I think it is an important way of finding out about each other.

Many of the Famous People are famous because they represent basic elements of the human race. They are stock characters. If we delve into the history of mime, we find the Greeks and Romans, thousands of years ago, had stock character mimes. The old man, the young lovers, the clever slave. . .all these characters were immediately recognizable to their audiences. The moment a stock character entered the stage with his particular walk, everyone cheered or booed accordingly.

Stock Character Walks

In mime there are several stock walks that children can learn and appreciate. I usually start by making them aware of the movements of people around them — their family, friends, people at school. Suppose we saw these people for the first time — what would we know about them by the way they moved? If you see your mother from a great distance, how do you know it is she?

With many stock characters the walk, the body movement, is governed by their personality, by the part of the body that matters most for them. The children have great fun trying all these different walks in many different situations. I practice the different walks with background music. I send the children in search of music that will help establish the rhythm of each personality. I've listed some suggestions for music on records or tape, but you can also accompany the children yourself on the piano, or any other musical instrument, or a group of children could form a rhythm band and play appropriate music.

The FAT PERSON walks from the *stomach*. Relax back on the heels and let that big tummy direct all your movements. Watch *Zero Mostel*. . .a well-padded *Santa Claus*. . .*Jackie Gleason*. . .*W.C. Fields*. . .*Hardy* (of Laurel and Hardy). . .*Robert Morley*. . .*Archie Bunker*. . . *Fat Albert*.

Good music: Chinese Dance from Nutcracker Suite; the Grandfather theme from *Peter and the Wolf*.

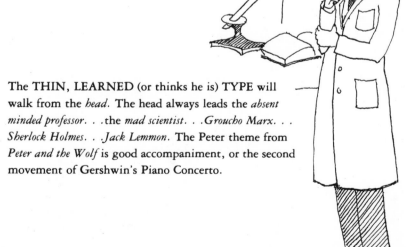

The THIN, LEARNED (or thinks he is) TYPE will walk from the *head*. The head always leads the *absent minded professor*. . .the *mad scientist*. . .*Groucho Marx*. . . *Sherlock Holmes*. . .*Jack Lemmon*. The Peter theme from *Peter and the Wolf* is good accompaniment, or the second movement of Gershwin's Piano Concerto.

The TOUGH GUY. . .the one who is in charge of the action. . . knows that all his strength is in his *shoulders*. He is always ready for a fight, always quick on the draw. He will move from the shoulders, letting them dictate to the rest of the body, like *John Wayne*. . . *The Fonz*. . .*Burt Lancaster*. . .*Clint Eastwood*. . .*Mohammed Ali*.

Use the Wolf theme from *Peter and the Wolf*.

The UNDERDOG, the little man, or woman, will move from the *heels*. He is not sure that he should be there, and may have to scamper away if the Fat Man or the Tough Guy appears on the scene. Look at *Edith Bunker*. . .*Charlie Chaplin*. . .*Laurel* (of Laurel and Hardy). . .*Woody Allen*. . *Jerry Lewis*.

Any blues music makes good accompaniment.

The PROUD will walk from the *nose*, literally looking down their noses at the rest of the world. *Generals*, and many people in high office have cultivated this special walk. George C. Scott did a perfect job in the film *Patton. Kings* and *Queens*, and even good old *Uncle Sam* have all acquired the "I-am-above-you" walk.

There is another group who walk from the nose, but this time the nose pokes out horizontally, like the *Wicked Witch of the West* or any kind of *snoopy-nosy guy*.

Accompany with any military march or the overture to *Guys and Dolls*.

Rimsky-Korsakoff's *Scheherazade* or the theme from the *Sting* is appropriate.

The OLD MAN OR WOMAN. As a person grows older the center of gravity slowly moves down from the upper chest area, sometimes almost to the *knees* (in a very elderly or feeble person). When working on this particular walk, start young, with an imaginary force somewhere under the throat, and slowly let it move down, affecting shoulders, back, stomach, feet. . .every part of your body, until you have the stock Old Man (or Woman) of Greek and Roman times.

I've used the Neptune movement from Holst's *The Planets* and the Beatles' "Goodbye Old Friends."

The **YOUNG** and **ALLURING**, (the "Soubrette") will acquire a sexy walk from the *pelvis* (after all, that is "where it's at" for them.) So let the hips be the moving force, in walking, in sitting, in all movements — not just by swinging them from side to side, but by moving them forward too, like *Farrah Fawcett-Majors. . .Mae West. . .Zsa Zsa Gabor. . .Elvis Presley. . .Tom Jones.*

The **INGENUE**, or **HEROINE** is the "lady" or Mistress of the house. Apart from looking decorative, she also says, by her movements, "Don't Touch." She walks from her *toes,* and sometimes also from her *finger-tips,* according to the time in which she lives. Well-known ingenues include *Julie Andrews. . .Ophelia. . .Melanie* (from *Gone with the Wind*). . .*Grace Kelly.*

The Don Juan theme from Richard Strauss is good music to mime a heroine by.

All these characters can do more than just walk if you put them in an interesting situation. In all character work, it is important that the different movements and the rhythm of the personality are sustained all the way through to the end of the scene. In mime, this is much easier to do than in a play or musical, because the whole focus is on the movement. When you add words or, even more difficult, songs, there are so many things to think about that the characterization is often lost, even in professional theatre.

Here are some places where different characters can interact in mime. Make sure, first, that the entrances and exits are strong and definite.

. A restaurant. You might try the Fat Man first in a very fancy restaurant, then the "greasy spoon" variety. Even as he enters the restaurant, the thought of food makes him feel better. Does he pick a booth or a chair? Which can he fit into better? Now he looks at the menu. . .what will he order today? What will he do while he waits for it to be prepared? And when the food comes, how will he eat? And drink? Finally it's time to squeeze past the table, pay the check, and leave.

. On board an ocean liner or an airplane.

. At a sidewalk sale.

. The waiting room at the dentist or doctor.

. At the movies. What kind of film is being shown?

. At a swimming pool.

. The place where driving tests and motor vehicle inspections are given.

. On the beach.

A Simple Word Give a Clue to a Character For Young Children

I've borrowed this list of names from the English "Mr. Books" by Roger Hargreaves. These delightful stories are now available in America and all of them are good for character work with little children. The stories spring naturally from the personality involved. Mr. Messy, for example, keeps himself, his room, his house and his yard in utter chaos, until Mr. Clean comes along and takes him over.

. Mr. Bump	. Mr. Snow	. Mr. Noisy
. Mr. Daydream	. Mr. Bounce	. Mr. Small
. Mr. Funny	. Mr. Dizzy	. Mr. Chatterbox
. Mr. Happy	. Mr. Fussy	. Mr. Forgetful
. Mr. Lazy	. Mr. Impossible	. Mr. Greedy
. Mr. Muddle	. Mr. Mean	. Mr. Jelly
. Mr. Messy	. Mr. Tickle	. Mr. Topsy Turvy
. Mr. Sneeze	. Mr. Uppity	

My only complaint about these marvelous stories (and my daughters agree): where are the Mrs. . .Miss. . .or Ms. books? Naturally, you can change the names as you wish. The pictures accompanying the little books give excellent ideas for movement. All the stories lend themselves very well to acting out in pantomime with kindergarteners and first graders.

How Clothes And Costumes Affect Character Movement

The body shape and center of gravity will also be affected by the kind of clothes the character wears. People move differently when they put on clothes to do a dirty job, or dress up to go to a party.

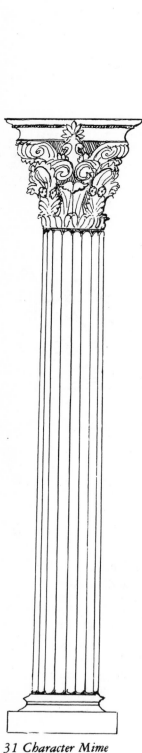

In a play, the children will be wearing costumes, and most of the time, that is exactly what it looks like: a costume. The trick is to make the audience believe the costumes are *clothes*, belonging to the character.

In pantomime, more often, the costumes and props are imaginary, just like everything else. However, many famous mimes will use just one property, or article of clothing, to give us a clue to their characters. Marcel Marceau adds a top hat with a flower as he evolves the delightful character Bip.

I have found older grades to be fascinated by the history of costume and its effect on movement. The historian James Laver says that our whole life style is reflected in the shape of the things we wear and use.

The Greeks, Romans, And Biblical Times: 500 B.C. - 1000 A.D.

This culture evolved around the Mediterranean, in a hot, dry, hilly terrain always close to the Mediterranean Sea. Clothes were protection from hot sun, because most of life was lived outdoors. The freedom of thought that grew out of the discipline of ancient Greece and the Roman Empire is reflected in everything they used.

Look at the picture of typical Greek and Roman clothes, and note the graceful folds of the toga or chiton, allowing for free, easy, natural movements.

Drape a sheet around the child and let him get used to moving with plenty of air around him, in bare feet or sandals.

31 Character Mime

Medieval Times: 1000 A.D. - 1500 A.D.

The Church held sway, and men and women aspired to loftier thoughts and deeds. An age of great chivalry and great class distinction, from the King, downwards.

For richer people, more elaborate costume. A great many cloaks, many of which trail on the ground behind the wearer. We are not used to wearing cloaks and trains, and their mis-use can be unsightly. How many brides have you seen, hitching up their train in an ugly fashion as they mounted the steps or pulled themselves into a car? Medieval people were accustomed to letting things hang about them, and letting the clothes follow the movement of the wearer. They held their heads high, and displayed their elegant sleeves by keeping their elbows away from the body.

Hands were held low down, and people greeted one another with a hand clasp (not shake) and a bow.

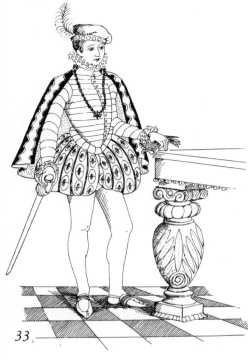

Renaissance: 1500 - 1650

An adventurous far-reaching age when new discoveries in every field excited the eye, the ear, the mind. Queen Elizabeth I, Galileo, Leonardo da Vinci, Shakespeare all wore clothes like these, and used accessories like these.

These adventurous people stood as if poised to go — hands on hip (and sword), knees bent, thin-soled shoes or high boots, ready for action. With all that lace and those high ruffs, no wonder the Three Musketeers swaggered through life. The lady should move in her great skirts like a Spanish galleon in full sail.

18th Century

With the Bicentennial year behind us, we have all witnessed many 20th century people looking very odd and uncomfortable in frilly caps and tri-corner hats and knee breeches. Yet if we look at the many pictures of the period we see that Alexander Hamilton wears his wig as comfortably as we wear a T-shirt. The men wished to exhibit a fine leg (the stocking and breeches helped to do this), so the 18th century gentleman should walk with zest, his pleated coat tails swinging out behind him, and the muscles of his leg well displayed in front. You've seen today's women and girls looking bowed down under the Martha Washington cap, as if Independence was something they had never heard of.

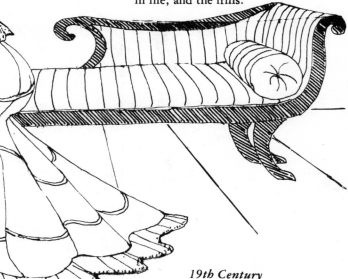

The 18th-century woman held her head high, her back straight, and moved easily and definitely, skirts swishing besides her.

George Washington lived in the age of reason and clear thinking, but also the Pursuit of Happiness, so he enjoyed the good things in life, and the frills.

19th Century

The Victorian era was named after the lady who reigned supreme. When Queen Victoria went into mourning for Prince Albert, so did the rest of the world. Men have not really recovered from Albert's death; the dark suit persists to this day. Our great great grandparents looked a lot like the sofas they sat upon.

Victorian and Edwardian costume did extraordinary things to the shape of the human body. Remember how Scarlett O'Hara was laced into a ridiculous corset, and how our great-grandfathers endured the stiffest high starched collar on the hottest day? Show the children photographs from that era, and they will give many ideas for stance and movement. In those days, richer children were taught deportment, and little girls had to walk about with books on their heads, while little boys suffered in starched sailor suits. It was not until the 19th century that special clothing was made for children. Before that, children wore a miniature version of adult dress.

Men dominated women in this age of the strict Papa and so walked with cane and top hat as if they ruled the world (they did!) Women were supposed to be "ladies," so tripped along in their crinolines, with eyes slightly downcast. The hand shake was quite high in the air.

20th Century

From 1920 onwards the straight lines — the square — the utility look came in. Various wars have left their stamp, but it is the machine that wins out in everything.

When men and women were finally freed of their corsets, after World War I, the 1920's brought a much more relaxed way of moving. The military styles of the 1940's tightened us up just a little, but by the time we reached the blue-jeans and long hair of the 1960's, movement had become not just relaxed, but positively sloppy. We no longer greet one another — physically. The bow and curtsey are part of another generation, where people had more time than "Hi!" allows.

Origins Affect Movement Too

I once boarded a subway in London, and was confronted by a carload of identically-dressed, stiff, black-coated, bowler-hatted, umbrella-clad English businessmen. Suddenly the door opened, and a West Indian in bright blue suit and pink striped vest and the craziest little hat walked through the train, hips swinging, singing a little song to himself. He brought a wealth of Jamaican sunshine and warmth to that foggy day in London town.

People move differently if they constantly walk in the sun, or stoop in rice fields, or huddle against the rain and the wind. An Indian lady in a sari, an African in a dashiki, a Scotsman in a kilt, all will move as the dress and climate dictate.

Do black people move differently from whites? Do Arabs walk differently from Chinese? It is all worthy of discussion with an interested group of children. Temperament, too, will play its part in movement. Some races speak with their hands. Ask the children to demonstrate a typical Italian gesture, or a Jewish gesture, or Spanish or English or whatever.

Age

Most 10-year-olds will not always be playing their own age in mime classes, or in plays. When they play different ages, they do so in a fairly superficial way: a young person walks upright; an older one is bent over and uses a stick. I think it is a good idea to let the children observe the movements of different age groups. If you are waiting in a public place, play the "How old do you think he/she is?" game.

A good mime lesson to teach age can be done through birthdays. While they are concentrating on conveying age, let the children be themselves. It is too complicated to add other elements of characterization, and anyway character building should be done gradually. Here is the birthday game:

Show me what you would do from the time you woke up in the morning on your

- 1st birthday
- 5th birthday
- 16th birthday
- 40th birthday
- 80th birthday.

The children will be quick to tell you that people do not always look their age. Discuss things that make a difference. Here are some exercises for people who look younger, or older, than their actual age:

- A 10-year-old pickpocket and beggar, underfed, but sharp-eyed and "old" for his age, going about his stealthy business like a hardened criminal ten years older.

- A 90-year-old lady from Georgia in Russia, who lives on yoghurt and vegetables, and still works in the vineyards, picking grapes. She looks 25 years younger.

- A 50-year-old retired boxer. He used to be a great champion, but now he has nothing to do, so he eats too much and gets very bored just pottering about the garden, thinking of the "good old days."

- The Hunchback of Notre Dame, only about 25, but so deformed, and deaf from the constant noise of the bells, that he appears much older as he tries to make dinner for Esmeralda, the gypsy girl he loves.

The children may bring more examples from real life.

"Seeing" The Character In the Mind's Eyes

Just as they did using the glass ball in Chapter III, the children can really think hard about portraying a character. Children can take turns to describe a person to the rest of the group. This is easiest when the character they are describing is someone they know, but they can also make up an imaginary person, or choose someone from a book or a movie. At this stage of the game, you can encourage them to bring in fantasy characters. Our literature is full of such weird and wonderful characters, . . .the Hobbit, the Wizard of Oz, the talking beasts of C.S. Lewis's Narnia, characters from comic strips and cartoons. While one child talks, the rest of the class will sit quietly, trying to "see" the character before beginning to move. Here's a description that stimulated an extraordinary session in character movement:

> You are an old, old lady, all bent over and crooked, with horrible pointed fingernails and dirty, evil-looking hands. You have broken spectacles on the end of your long nose, and your teeth are all black and falling out. That raggedy old cloak trailing behind you is your only dress, and your sharp pointed shoes are are full of magic and holes. You have never taken a shower in your whole life, and bats and eels are your favorite foods. You are happiest when you're flying through the air on your broomstick. Because you are so ugly, no one wanted to marry you, so you have no children, and you give all your love to that mangy old black cat who sleeps in your bed and shares your supper. When you climb through the cobwebs to your secret room full of spells, it is the beginning of another witchy day. Get busy — it is time to go!
>
> Annalise, Age 11

"I think I could turn and live with animals. They do not sweat and whine about their condition. They do not lie awake in the dark and weep for their condition. Not one is respectable or unhappy over the whole earth," said Walt Whitman. While I respect his feelings of frustration with the human race (who hasn't had that feeling?), I would like to take him to task on one essential issue: we cannot "turn and live with animals" — we *are* animals.

Our Animal Heritage in Language and Symbol

My own thinking is that we should turn and live with the *good* animal instincts inside us. Our animal kinship has crept into our language; we preen like peacocks, fight like cat and dog — take to water like a fish, race like horses, run like a hare. Millions of people live their lives closely involved with cats and dogs — bugs and birds, cows and chickens, roaches and rats. All the arts have — while "holding the mirror up to nature" — seen animals reflected very clearly in that mirror of life.

Children, in particular, have an affinity and fascination for the animal world. We, as adults, have understood this, and filled our children's books with animals who behave like people. From Beatrice Potter to Walt Disney to Richard Scarry our children, in the last 100 years, have been swamped with a host of animals, none of them truly animal.

Our babies can often make animal talk before they use words. My own son could say "woof woof" and "miawau" long before he said, "Mommy". One thought occurs to me as I flick through the pages of children's books with the adorable bunnies in frock coats and little pigs with hats and coats: we are indeed the sons and daughters of the great god Pan.

We recognize in him the wild yet joyous nature we call "animal." A gang of children, let out from school for recess, will behave more like the goat Pan, than the human side of his nature. Even in modern urban life, where our only encounter with animals may be a trip to the zoo, we all share an animal/human heritage. There is a large gorilla at the Bronx Zoo, with a very superior air, and a steadfast stare for all human observers. I have the strongest sensation when I see this animal. Who is looking at whom? Which of us is really in the zoo, as an object of curiosity, the gorilla or me?

Look at the man/animal hybrid from the old Stone Age on the frontispiece of the first chapter. "How much of me is truly me, how much the horn and the tail?" the creature seems to ask. Centuries from now, an archeologist examining the ruins of Disney World could well conclude that some god-like king, called Mickey Mouse, must have reigned in our civilization. Who was this mouse in short pants whose emblem we find stamped on everything everywhere?

Civilizations in the past have made animals into essential symbols:

. The bull: the essence of the male force, and the cow as the symbol of fertility and maternity;

. The cat — as a superior, priestly, mysterious, animal;

. The eagle as the symbol of strength and lofty ideals; the dove stands for peace, the hawk for war;

. The rat, maligned throughout literature, a threat to man's survival even today, and now condemned to suffer as chief martyr for all kinds of scientific experiments.

Mime Helps Children To Discover The Real Animal World

As part of their civilization, their education, I think it is important that children understand more about the animal kingdom than a pet puppy for Christmas, or Donald Duck, or Miss Piggy can afford.

Imitating the movements of animals is an occupation as old as man. Children are very good at it — perhaps because they are closer to the creeping-on-all-fours stage than adults — and yet we very seldom give them the opportunity to explore this natural talent. Worse still, I have encountered many teachers who expect their children to imitate their bad imitation of the animal, rather than letting the child find his or her own creation. "Let's all be elephants," says the benevolent teacher, "Now everyone watch me. Here's my trunk," and she waves one arm in the air and drops to her knees — so do 25 other "elephants." No one is anywhere near an elephant. Yet I have seen a four-year-old with an uncanny elephant-like feeling: the heaviness, the slow swinging body, the movement of the head, (with trunk, incidentally, invisible, yet somehow very visible to the imagination of the child and to me.) This four-year-old may never have seen a real elephant, but from pictures and some innate feeling for the animal, he managed to catch something extraordinarily real.

Focusing On The Essential Movements And Rhythms

Work on animals at any level comes from association and observation. A good time to begin work on animals is after

. A visit to a zoo, or a farm;

. Viewing a movie about animals;

. Having the animal enthusiast in the group share his pictures and stories;

. Bringing in a pet to show the children.

In your discussion, focus on the way the animal moves — what is the most important part of the body to move? For monkeys, it may be the arms, totally relaxed, swinging from the shoulders. For the cat, it may be the back and the tail sinuously undulating. An owl hardly moves at all — unless flying. It sits with an almost constipated intensity, the feathers hunched around the non-existent neck; and the occasional blinking of the eyes, will tell us the bird is alert. Each animal has a rhythm all its own. Anyone visiting a zoo where different animals are gathered side by side will sense this changing mood, from the glowering stillness of the bored tiger, the chattering swinging swiftness of the monkeys, on past the slow inert movement of the turtles, on to the aviary, full of humming birds, twittering, flying so fast, so free.

Having set the scene for your animal mimes, you are ready for some action. I like to let children show me their own sense of rhythm for various animals. Some children have a particularly sharp sense for this work. They may not do so well in other areas of mime. They may not do well in *anything* — but they *are* good at being animals. Perhaps an extra dose of animal affinity handed down from the great god, Pan??

In order to achieve true creativity, and not a host of "copy cats," I like to start with everyone well spaced out in the room — each with his or her own private creativity area. I find a good way to warm up is to go through many different animals: birds, fish and insects, freezing between each one, so that the body and the mind have a moment to change gear and find a new rhythm.

This poem* is great for small children —

> Frogs jump
> Caterpillars hump
> Worms wiggle
> Bugs jiggle
> Rabbits hop
> Horses clop
> Snakes slide
> Seagulls slide
> Mice creep
> Deer leap
> Puppies bounce
> Kittens pounce
> Lions stalk —
> But
>   I WALK!

40 Animal Mime

**"Jump or Jiggle" by Evelyn Beyer from *Another Here and Now Storybook* by Lucy Sprague Mitchell, E.P. Dutton & Co, 1937.

With older children, just try a good mixture —

. Squirrels looking for nuts;

. Snake climbing a wall;

. Vulture hovering over its prey;

. Hungry dinosaur in primeval forest;

. A seal at the zoo feeding time and show time;

. A flamingo, in and out of water;

. A turtle — very old — but interested in something new;

. A bear, waking up in spring after hibernation and looking for food;

. A fly trying to get out of a spiderweb;

. Pigs in mud.

Camille Saint-Saens understood the difference between animal characteristics — and in "Carnival of the Animals" captured the rhythm so well. You may wish to use some of this music for your first few lessons.

Dealing With Noise

It is almost impossible for small children to become the animal, without accompanying noise. However, a word of caution. Have you ever watched a group of children becoming lions and tigers? The fun of making so much noise often precludes everything else, so that the group will sacrifice the good strong cat-like movements for just a roar. Besides, it is phony; tigers and lions have a majestic silence about them, unless aroused to roar. I think the simplest way round the animal noise problem is to find the animal in silence, and then to add a situation, such as hunger or attack, and *then* add the sound. This way, there is motivation for the animal sounds, so they may produce even better roaring.

Concentrating on a Particular Animal

After the introductory lesson with animal rhythms — all different — I feel most children are ready to concentrate on *truly* becoming one particular animal. The rest of the chapter is divided into sections on animals — (mammals, reptiles, and amphibians); birds; insects; fish; strange animals — (prehistoric, imaginary, monsters).

I usually start with monkeys, because

. I believe in the Darwinian theory of evolution;
. Children love monkeys;
. People do well what comes easily —

Monkeys comprise may different families: gorillas, apes, gibbons, chimpanzees, baboons, macaques, and other lesser known species. Most monkeys have longer arms than humans, and the orang-utan puts its knuckles to the ground and swings its body between its long arms, using them like crutches. A good trick if you can do it! Gibbons hold their long arms over their heads when walking and all monkeys do so much swinging from the trees, in most species, the arms are much more powerful than the legs. Ask the children to bring in monkey pictures — provide some yourself — and stories — and then talk about their environment. Where do they live? What do they eat? Where,

41 Animal Mime

and how, do they sleep? What do monkeys do all day in the jungle? What is it like to be covered with fur, to have a tail, to swing through the air?

Now curl up asleep in your favorite place. The sun is just coming up. You have had a very good night's sleep — What can you hear all about you at this time of the morning? Listen — who is nearby — who is far away? Now something in your stomach says "I'm hungry'" — so go and look for food. It is quite difficult to find food today. What happens to you — before you come across something — delicious — a banana or a coconut? Enjoy your food — but remember — we are in the jungle, so be careful, someone else may want your food — keep your ears and eyes open. You have not quite finished your meal — when you meet another monkey. Will you share your food? Fight? Play? Chase? Or groom one another?

By now you should have a room full of monkeys, enjoying the freedom of life in the jungle. When the monkeys are truly monkeys, I like to keep the character, but change the environment.

1. Suddenly freeze. The monkeys have all been taken to a large monkey house in a zoo in the northern part of America. It is *much* colder than the jungle. There is a large cage. All these strange people are constantly looking at you. How will you behave in this situation? Do you like the food? Are you bored, hungry, unhappy, ready to amuse the crowd? Most of all, what do you feel about the bars that surround you?

(I did this exercise in a gym, which happened to have a large mural, mostly of Bicentennial people, on one of the walls. We used the mural as the crowd of people in the zoo, and I defined the limits of the cage within the red lines on the gymnasium floor.)

2. A famous circus is passing by. They decide to hold tryouts for the monkey show with all the monkeys in the cage. They leave clothes, bicycles, baseball and bat, a table set with a meal, rhythm band instruments, umbrellas, hats, purses. . . all kinds of things. Then the trainer watches for the monkeys he can best use in his act.

Use either real or imaginary clothes and props. The Circus man can pick the monkeys he wants to use in his trapeze act, birthday party, bicycle act, or ball game.

3. These same circus monkeys, now used to performing for people and living in the human world — have suddenly been taken back to the jungle. The truck they were travelling in stops in the middle of the jungle. The monkeys are still wearing their funny human clothes, and they have brought along some of their props.

(Here I divide the class in half)

The jungle monkeys — — those that have never seen a human — — are amazed. What happens when the back of the truck opens and the two groups of monkeys confront one another?

By the end of this session, the children will have been sustaining the character of a monkey throughout quite a lengthy period of time. I find that many children have developed personalities for their monkeys. After an "in depth" approach like this, it is pretty tame stuff to just "be a monkey." You know monkeys. You have been there.

THE SQUIRREL

Whisky, Frisky,
Hippity hop,
Up he goes
to the tree top!

Whirly, twirly,
Round and round
Down he scampers
to the ground.

Furly, curly,
What a tail!
Tall as a feather,
Broad as a sail!

Where's his supper?
In the shell.
Snappy, cracky,
Out it fell.

Unknown

With younger children, perhaps you begin by studying a real cat. You look at its movements, talk about it. Now you are ready to become a cat — out on the street. The street is full of cats — all very hungry.

You head for the garbage cans and after making a big mess, you find some delicious tidbits on the bottom of the can. Someone human comes along and chases you away — just when you are enjoying yourself. You find a good hiding place and lick your paws, rub ears and whiskers and lick all the dainty morsels from your fur. Suddenly you look up at the cat next door — your old enemy! Slowly the two walk around one another, and then have a lovely cat fight! Suddenly — you freeze as you hear the sound of your mutual enemy, the big dog down the street. Scatt!! Up a tree, where you hiss and spit and fluff up your fur. You stay up in the tree till night. When all is safe, you climb down the tree, and look around for something to eat. It is dark, but you can see everything with your marvellous cat's eyes — and you have seen — a mouse!

Any teacher who has ever known a cat will be able to continue the scenario at length. The children will mime this story as you tell it.

If you use a poem, I think it is best to read the poem first, and then let the children give their own interpretation of the animal in the poem. Here are some good ones:

THE SPIDER*

With black, wicked eyes, hairy thin legs and
           creepy crawly movements
Black shoe polish coat shining dully.
Hairy black thin legs.
Beautiful, silky and soft web
Dew hangs like miniature diamonds on lacy fingers.
A quick movement and this monster disappears.

J. Jenkins, Age 10, New Zealand

LONE DOG

I'm a lean dog, a keen dog, a wild dog, and lone;
I'm a rough dog, a tough dog, hunting on my own;
I'm a bad dog, a mad dog, teasing silly sheep;
I love to sit and bay the moon, to keep fat souls from sleep.

I'll never be a lap dog, licking dirty feet,
A sleek dog, a meek dog, cringing for my meat,
Not for me the fireside, the well-filled plate,
But shut door, and sharp stone, and cuff and kick and hate.

Not for me the other dogs, running by my side,
Some have run a short while, but none of them would bide.
O mine is still the lone trail, the hard trail, the best,
Wide wind, and wild stars, and hunger of the quest!

Irene Rutherford McLeod

*From *Miracles,* ed. by Richard Lewis, Simon and Schuster. 1971.

A Mime Class Based On Pets

Each child choses his own pet — hamster, rabbit, mouse, dog, cat, turtle, pony, gerbil . . .the pet he/she owns or would like to own. They then become that animal — asleep at first. How does it sleep?

> Wake up and look for food. Do you play? How do you play? Along comes one of those two-footed creatures. How do you feel about them?

You may want to work in groups, or individually, with a kind of "show-and-tell" for each animal. I like to put groups of animals together in an interesting situation.

. For all the *dogs*. Your master (mistress is going away on vacation. You are being brought to a kennel. Do you like it? What do you think of all the other dogs? How are you treated?

. All the *guinea pigs* are in a cage — one cage. Somebody forgot to care for you. You are very dirty, hungry and thirsty. Which guinea pig is going to be the first to escape — and how?

. This is not a cage — it is a *Mouse* Palace, with every conceivable kind of swing, seesaw, hidey-hole, slide and ferris wheel. It's a Disney World for real mice!

. These *ponies* are all waiting in a big field. Today is the horse show and gymkhana. Who will jump the highest? Who will win the blue ribbon?

Non-Domestic Animals

If the interest in animal pantomime is still running high, you can explore .

. Animals who live in Arctic climates — dog teams of huskies; polar bears, in and out of icy water; caribou, and moose in Spring (when the ice is breaking up); wolves, silverfox, walruses; and — of course — seals. If you need "cold" music, Symphony No. 7 (Antarctica) by Vaughn Williams has howling winds and icy fiddles — highly suitable background music.

. Animals serving mankind — police dogs in training, camels crossing the desert, oxen ploughing the fields, donkeys on the high mountains.

. Jungle and Plains animals — tigers; lions; rhino, zebra; panthers. Use some of the class as hunters on safari with nets and cages. Are they out to shoot, or to capture?

. Wild animals of North America, before the white man came: skunks, beavers, otter, buffalo, raccoons, woodchucks, bears. All the animals are happy. It is spring. Some have just awoken from the deep sleep of winter. Streams are running, trees are budding. Man comes, bringing some kind of disaster. . .a forest fire, perhaps, or pollution to the water, or bulldozers and electric saws. The land is being used by man now, so you will have to go. The sign for disaster could be red lightning or red crepe paper strips for the forest fire. Use a tape recording of noises that say "Pollution" — a chance to make very disgusting sounds — legitimately! Or electric saw sounds, again on the tape recorder.

. Reptiles and amphibians: alligators in the Everglades of Florida; turtles, lizards, worms. Be careful! A fisherman is after you. He needs you for his bait. Snakes; frogs; tadpoles. Set up different ponds or swamps and areas of land between them. All these animals are very hungry, until a helicopter flies over the land and water, dumping a hundred loaves of bread. Use a helicopter noise (a hair dryer?) at the appropriate moment.

Developing a Full-Length Animal Mime Play

There are many stories available. One scenario (with animal masks) is on page 141, but you may also find your own among

. African folk tales (many of which concern animals)
. Indian myths and legends
. *Just So Stories and The Jungle Book,* by Rudyard Kipling
. *Mother West Wind's Animal Friends,* by Thornton Burgess
. *The Wind in the Willows,* by Kenneth Graham
. *Tales of Uncle Remus,* by Joel Chandler Harris

For mime I prefer stories where animals act more or less as animals to Babar the Elephant and cartoon animals like Felix the Cat and Bugs Bunny. Most of these animal characters are so human, they may as well speak. Save them for creative dramatics.

Birds

Peter Brook, the famous English theatre director, devised an improvised play where everyone was a bird, and only bird language was used. It was a fascinating and absorbing theatrical experience, lasting over two hours with not one word spoken. The improvised story was developed, I gather, through the characteristics of the different species of birds.

When I want to mime birds, I take the children outside first, to look up and about for various birds and their flying styles. Even more interesting is a visit to an aviary, or a wildlife sanctuary. A good project for a more experienced, or older, group would be for each student to study one particular bird.

When I directed the play, The Tingalary Bird (a magical, not a "real" bird), the boy who played the Bird visited the local zoo to find one bird that could give him ideas for movement and character in this role. We searched the zoo for the "right" bird, and I shall never forget the moment when Jim suddenly spotted "THE" bird (a species of hawk). "That's it!" he cried. Every day, Jim came back to the zoo to visit "his" bird, to see it under different circumstances. The boy and the bird developed quite a relationship.

All children have seen ducks, swans and geese, so to start your "bird work" set up a pond area in your acting space. Let the children decide if they are ducks, ducklings, swans or geese. Let them huddle together on the bank first because it is night time.

Dawn comes. Who will be first into the pond? How do you walk on dry land? How do you swim? Here come the children, throwing bread. Who will get the largest piece? Who gets nothing at all. Now it is beginning to rain. . .

(You can use rain sounds here)

What a wonderful time the ducks are having, but the children have gone home with their coats over their heads. It was only a shower. The rain stops. The Canadian geese were only visiting on their way South — now they all gather together in formation and fly away — honking their "good-byes" to the ducks and swans below.

Good Swan, Duck And Geese Stories To Mime

"The Ugly Duckling" by Hans Christian Andersen is an obvious choice. The Danny Kaye recording of the song is good for small children to act out. Try an Indian Duck

Dance with the older ones — or another Andersen story: "The Wild Swans" — a beautiful story for mime.

My favorite swan story is from the legend of Lohengrin. Richard Wagner has done a very good job of turning it into an opera, but the story has so much action, it would make a lovely mime play. The swan is really the central character in the original story.

We have some beautiful swan music available —

. Swan Lake, by Tchaikovsky. Pick your favorite piece in the music and mime the story. "The Dying Swan" (made famous by Anna Pavlova) is effective as a solo mime, as well as a dance.

. The Swan of Tuonela, by Sibelius, a Finnish legend with serene and lovely music.

. The Swan from The Carnival of the Animals, by Saint-Saens.

Here is a Goose story with plenty of action for the grade 5's, this time based on Roman history. In 390 B.C. the Gauls, a fierce and savage race, attacked the Romans and drove them to a steep rocky hill known as The Capital. On top of the Capital was a fort with many Roman soldiers. The night of the invasion, the Consul of the Fort, Manlius, was awakened by the cackling of the sacred geese in the temple of Zeus. Rushing to the wall of the Capital, Manlius saw that the Gauls had already climbed it. (Use an imaginary wall — good occupational mime). He ran to wake up the soldiers in the fort. They came to the wall, and defeated the Gauls. (Good death scenes here — as wounded soldiers fall back down the hill!) The sacred geese, it is said, aided the Roman soldiers in their attack by pecking at the Gauls.

Sound effects — perhaps some percussion instruments — make an excellent accompaniment to this story.

"If You Were A Bird, What Species Would You Be?"

We know that Nina in Chekhov's play, The Seagull, felt herself to be a seagull. Keats and Shelley wrote some of their greatest poetry by projecting themselves into nightingales and skylarks. What species would you be? Would you live in a small cage? A large aviary? Or perched on a seaman's shoulder? Do you follow the ships, gliding with all the other birds. Perhaps you wade through water with long legs and long beak, and pull worms from the mud. Or do you peck at the trees with your sharp beak and find insects to eat? If you love cities, then you might be a pigeon. If you don't like to fly at all, perhaps you are a penguin. If I had my choice, I would be a brilliantly colored humming bird in the jungles of South America.

When you have chosen "your" bird, curl up very small. Every bird — every *body* — that comes to this earth has to be born. Let us imagine that you are very tiny inside the egg — growing a little bigger each day. Today is the greatest day in your life — your birth day. With your beak, make a tiny crack in the shell. Now make it larger, larger — large enough for you to break out of this shell into the big world beyond. Is it light out there? Can you see? What is that strange air all around you? Can you stand? Are you all alone — or is there someone much bigger than you to welcome you to this world? Perhaps to feed you? What do you think of your first taste of food? Now stretch your wings a little. Let us imagine you are having your first flying lesson. If you are a bird of prey you will learn how to swoop and hover. If you are a small bird you will learn how to flutter gently. If you are an ostrich, then forget the flying — you must learn how to run.

Once the flying lessons get started with your variety of birds, Respighi's music "The Birds" gives just the right background.

Insects

Many people are frightened of insects and see them as a curse on the human race. Insects eat billions of dollars worth of our food each year, and cause disease and discomfort. They can even eat their way through your house. Yet the honey bee, while looking for its own food, provides us with flowers and sweetness. Insect life is so varied, the life style of termites and bees so structured, and, above all, the movement of many insects so fascinating, that they are certainly worth a lesson in mime. I developed one called "The Life of the beautiful Monarch Butterfly" after the children had completed a study in science on the life of the caterpillar butterfly.

> Start life as an egg. . .very small. Develop slowly into a larva. You are now a caterpillar, stretching out your antennae. Bring them in again and curl up as a pupa, the third stage in your eventful life. Now, very, very slowly, complete your metamorphosis into the beautiful butterfly. Feel your lovely wings in the sunlight. Explore the world around you, and rest on a twig.

I then divided the group into pairs, one being the butterfly, the other the butterfly hunter, complete with net, pins, books, charts, whatever else he needed. The butterflies are free to fly happily around until the chase begins, but end up as part of a collection in a book.

The children were worried about the cruelty of this, so we reversed the procedure and let the (giant) butterfly carry off the hunter and put him/her in *his* collection.

A Scenario For An Insect Play

I had recently been through a session with the exterminator because my house had termites (I hope that is still the correct tense for the verb!) My own children were very interested in the hierarchy of the termite world, similar to that of the bee. I decided to have a Bee Colony for my next mime class. What competition for the role of the Queen! We divided the rest of the group into workers, drones, flowers, and THE enemy (we decided on a black bear.)

The Queen laid her eggs, fertilized by the drones, and the worker bees built the hive, collected the honey from the flowers, and stored it in the hive. The workers then set about making beeswax for the honeycomb, and the Queen laid more eggs in the cells of the honeycomb. All was going well, until the bear — a hungry bear — came looking for honey. The bees stung him, but he scooped up all the honey and sat there licking his paws.

Group Work On Insects

. The spider and the fly. . After spinning an elaborate web, the spider looks out for his first victim and manages to entice a fly into his web. Will he get free?

. A family of cockroaches are having a marvelous time in a dirty, unoccupied apartment, until the new tenants come in and attack with Raid!

. Who can jump the highest in the Insect Olympics?

The world famous Flea Circus — the cleverest performing fleas in the world!

Half the class becomes the fruit. (Let them choose their own variety.) The other half are the fruit flies, laying little eggs that become maggots and bore their way through the fruit, until a scientist comes along and takes all the fruit flies away for an experiment.

Fish

I think one of the best solo mimes I have ever seen was a 12-year-old boy — as a fish being caught, flipped onto the shore, gasping for breath and then thrown back into the water. It was a dynamic experience. The boy, incidentally, was labelled "backward" by educators.

Many children like to go fishing, and others have fish in an aquarium. Since the film "Jaws" I've noticed a great interest in sharks. Fish live in water — so I usually start my fish lessons by having the whole group at one end of the room. . .as people.

> This is the shallow part of the lake (or ocean, or river). Very slowly — the water is cold — we wade in, feeling that line of water moving up our bodies, until we submerge completely. We are fish! Water is our home. We can breathe with our gills; we can move through the water, swim down to the greatest depths. Enjoy the water.

This is the moment when I supply the bait for all the fish.

> Suddenly — you are hooked, brought up through the water, back into the air, and laid on the bank. You gasp for water. . .twist and flip. . .until the fisherman throws you back. Breathe again through your gills. Move your whole body with the motion of the water. You are home again.

Underwater Adventures In Mime

. A local pond is full of tadpoles. This poem, by 12-year-old William Michael Taylor, gives a good description:

> A tadpole, a baby slyful tadpole
> A tadpole, black and spotted tadpole
> A tadpole of speed and slenderness
> A tadpole with a glassy tail.
>
> She flips her tail and flashes on,
> She weaves her body about the weed,
> And jerks between a sharp great stone.
> She cuts the water of dirt and grit,
> And dyes the water with jump and vigor.
>
> She eats of weed, she eats of fly,
> She eats with fish, she eats with friend.
> At times of rest she sets her chest
> Upon the bed of sand and stone.
> Oh little tadpole, grow and grow again.*

These tadpoles are needed for the second grade science corner — So look out!

. The Aquarium. Who is the most beautiful fish and who the ugliest? Which fish likes to fight? How do they eat?

. The Ocean. Jelly fish, eels, flying fish, sharks, and flounder. It's the flounder the men with their nets want to catch. What adventures could they have?

*From *Miracles*, ed. by Richard Lewis, Simon and Schuster. 1971

- Ice fishing. If you are lucky enough to have different levels available in your working space, one level can be underwater; the other level the ice. Some children will be fishermen; others the fish.

- Underwater Expedition. Some children are divers looking for buried treasure, others the fish near this tropical island. Very unusual fish can be found here — flying fish that flip out of the water; walking fish, who have a set of legs and trundle along the ocean bed, and, of course, the deadly sword fish.

- Any good fishing stories, especially those the children in the group tell.

Strange Animals - Prehistoric, Extinct, And Monsters

It need hardly be said that today's child is mad about monsters. The most popular course at the local Saturday Fun School is Dinosaurs. I find that most children know more about these subjects than I — so I let *then* tell me what they would like to do. I introduce the subject with a discussion about prehistoric animals and how they might move. . .eat. . .sleep. . .fight. I throw in a few extinct animals like the Dodo Bird, the Sabre-Toothed Tiger, the bison and the mastodon. I then play a tape of very strange noises. (They sound prehistoric to me — I made the tape with junk lying around the house and some fiddling around with the speed controls on the tape recorder. Any sound will do!) At one point on the recorder the tape gets very loud. I ask the children what might be happening. These are some of the answers I have received:

- The huge, meat-eating allosauras attacks the plant-eating dinosaurs.

- The flying reptiles attack.

- Stone-age people are returning from the hunt when they are suddenly attacked by monsters who are hiding in the trees.

For large prehistoric animals two or three children may want to work together to become one huge dinosaur.

However, I still feel the best work with monsters is done with masks. For that, see Chapter X.

"Abstract mime" — a somewhat cold, empirical term for something which can be so dynamic. It encompasses all the world from a piece of cheese to the wind to the personification of Anger and Hate, Love and Boredom. Sensations, too. . .the response to tastes and smells and touch.

Anyone who comes into contact with children recognizes that their view of the world is more immediate, simpler, and much less "departmental" (to borrow a useful idea from Robert Frost!) than adults. Adults tend to think of movement in terms of occupational activity or imitating animals or people, and yet children's bodies can move equally well to the abstract world of things, devices, feelings, ideas, dress. Walk into the corridor of almost any elementary school, and the art work on the walls will be closer to Picasso than to Norman Rockwell. Just as children respond to abstract terms naturally through brightly colored paints, torn-up paper, glue, clay and rhythm band instruments, so they can also respond through movement.

Of all the different forms of mime, abstract mime benefits most from the use of percussion instruments, music, or sound effects. So prepare yourself with drums, cymbals, tamborine, record player, and tape recorder.

The World of Nature

Start with seeds. Using the entire group, let everyone begin very small, beneath the earth, in the dark. Slowly send forth a little green shoot; reach up for the light, grow bigger into the sun. . .the rain. . .the wind. . .to become —

. a beautiful rosebud; then a full blown rose, slowly losing its petals, and finally becoming just a stalk.

. a very prickly, strangely-shaped cactus in the hot desert sand.

. a weed, pushing its way through a crack in a city sidewalk.

. a Venus fly-trap, as an insect buzzes by.

. the reddest apple on a tree during an apple raid.

. a maple tree "helicopter" on a windy day.

. a piece of seaweed washed up on the beach.

Or act out, in groups, the life story of different trees. . .a Christmas tree farm. . .an old, old oak. . .a Canadian pine tree, used for lumber. . .a cypress tree in Florida.

Expand each idea by exploring the effects of different elements, light and darkness, people and animals, tools, knives, whatever comes into contact with the tree or plant. The road to a classroom where I used to teach mime followed a river bank that was lined with the most interesting trees, all bending in different ways toward the sun and the river. I let each child become any one of those trees, and lined them up on our own "river bank." First we very slowly grew into the shape of the tree; then we found out what it was like to be that tree at different seasons of the year. Finally the river flooded, and the trees were uprooted (to terrible sounds on the drum and cymbals). Branches broke off; lightening struck. The trees ended up as pieces of driftwood in the Forestry Museum.

Of course you may also borrow from the ballet and let fantastic things happen. A wood full of trees, on the stroke of midnight, might all come alive and dance. Once the plants in our Flower Shop uprooted themselves and explored the store. The owner talked to the plants too much! (We used a tape recorded voice on a too-fast speed.) Eventually they escaped to a quieter environment.

There are also many opportunities for work with fruit and vegetables. As with the work on animals, it is important for the child to create the *feeling* of the tree or plant, rather than trying to make the body look like one. I remember seeing a very clever carrot costume which was perfectly fine for a costume parade, but nowhere near as "carroty" as the non-costumed carrot I had in my "Vegetables and Fruits at the Supermarket" mime. This one made scrunchy noises, objected to boiling water, and hated the thought of his top being cut off and the smell of the onion next door!

The Elements Are Also Part of Nature

There must be hundreds of little plays and readers featuring Jack Frost, the Wind, the Sun and the Rain. In a sadly unimaginative first grade play, I remember that the only way we knew the Wind had entered was because he wore a placard around his neck with "WIND" written on it, and recited his two lines in a high monotone. Surely the Wind is movement, movement, movement! Here, with some appropriate sound effects, the children can *truly* become the blustering, boisterous wind. . .or the soft, gentle breeze, or the terrifying typhoon. Legends and myths give us innumerable stories about the elements. Here are some ideas I have used:

. "Roll yourself up into a ball of heat — the hottest thing in the Universe: the *Sun*. Feel all the rays darting from your body to the earth beneath. Come up slowly above the horizon and gradually send out more and more heat. Remember that the Sun also spins like a giant flaming top. At the clash of a cymbal, radiate sun-spots — so violent they jam the radio stations on earth far below."

"What happens to you on that extraordinary day of an eclipse?" I used one tall boy in a flowing dark cloak, passing shadows over all of us.

. Study the different *planets* that make up our universe. Each one has special characteristics. Gustav Holst's *The Planets* conveys a very good description of each planet. . .up to Pluto. A new planet has recently been discovered, so if you want to be precise, search for some far-out eerie sound for this latest planet. If you have enough space, set out the solar system (including the moons of Jupiter), in the correct order, all over the floor, allowing plenty of orbiting space. You may wish to add newer elements of outer space, like flying saucers, space ships, rockets and missiles.

. I believe that mime is one way for children to begin to understand *volcanoes* . . . *earthquakes*. . .*hurricanes,* and other disasters that pose difficult questions. Words seem so inadequate when children confront you with such questions as "Why did all these thousands of people die in the earthquake?" Perhaps the only answer is in the abstract — or through stories. Many children have felt better about hurricanes since

Dorothy was swept away to the land of Oz. These days we are all bombarded with disasters through television, film, and newspapers. Children watching the devastation of a tornado on the 6 o'clock news need some outlet for their feelings. It is one reason for the popularity of such movies as "Jaws" and "Earthquake."

I encourage the children to make their own sound effects for the following exercise. My students have taken some from a 99-cents Sound Effects record, and made earthquake sounds by clashing various objects close to the microphone of a tape recorder.

"Imagine you are a seething mass of heat and energy, deep in the bowels of the earth. Nature tells you to erupt, force your way through the rock. . .the soil, until finally you erupt, destroying buildings, ripping through streets, creating new mountains, rumbling through the valleys until slowly you die away."

I group the children into one large, hissing underground mass to begin, then, on a signal from "Nature," the earthquake slowly begins its path of destruction. We use the entire room, and designate imaginary mountains, buildings, lakes and streets in different areas. As the earthquake slowly subsides back into itself, the hissing dies out, there is stillness and silence for a few moments, and then the rumbling of stones, the crash of buildings.

Earth. . .In many creative drama exercises the children take journeys over different kinds of terrain. This time they *become* the terrain, in all its various forms. . .old, smooth, mossy rocks. . .sharp, craggy outcroppings. . .the desert sand in a sandstorm, squelchy mud. . .an overgrown garden full of thorny plants and tangly weeds. . .a whole range of mountains, using the entire class.

Water. . .I have so many good water lessons, I do not know where to start. Water is so flexible, and takes so many different forms. Here are a few suggestions:

1. The life of a river, running from its source, through waterfalls, dams, dry beds, and valleys, finally ending in the sea.

2. Underground springs, perhaps the hot water variety, hissing and spitting and bubbling out of the ground.

3. Oceans, under different circumstances: very calm and warm, laden with ice, polluted with oil from a tanker, raging in a terrible storm.

4. Icebergs, floating through the water near Greenland.

5. Stalactites and Stalagmites. (We used the constant drip-drop sound I remembered hearing in some caves in Bermuda.)

6. A tidal wave.

7. The life cycle of water. . .gathering in heavy, moisture-filled clouds. . .rain. . . freezing on ice-capped mountains. . .melting into waterfalls. . .streams. . .rivers. . . finally the big reservoir.

I usually follow my Water lessons with *Fire.* Most schools have fire drills, so children are quite accustomed to talking about fire. Now they have the opportunity to become the Fire itself. Start with the birth of a tiny flame, working its way through two twigs, and then gradually build up momentum, joining with other flames to burn down a whole forest.

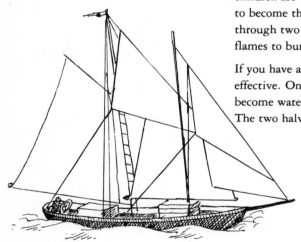

If you have access to any kind of stage lighting, some red flickering lights are most effective. Once the fire is successfully established, divide the group into two. Half become water. . .rain, or the water in the fire hoses; the other half are the fire. The two halves meet.

Machines Are Another Form of Abstract Mime

Most dramatics teachers will have used machines. The most popular way to begin is for one child to become the first part of the machine — a cog, a wheel, a piston, a spring — using her body in a rhythmic series of movements. Another child joins the first, with a different movement, and then a third. Gradually, the entire class joins in to become a vast, complex machine. It is an activity which always seems to succeed.

In a serious mime class, I think we can expand the idea of machines much further. I usually start quite freely by letting the children pantomime many different mechanical devices, so they can explore a whole range of body movements. Domestic appliances are fun. . .vacuum cleaners, electric blenders and mixers, garbage disposal units, lawn mowers, electric can openers, washing machines, carpet scrubbers, electric knives or saws, whistling tea kettles.

54 Abstract Mime

As machines often make a noise, the children may add their own appropriate sound effects. We think of mime as the Silent Art, because no words are used, but mime artists for centuries have accompanied their art with music and sound effects. Mime with utterance has been part of the European scene for many years. Besides, it is almost impossible for a child to become a train without sounding like one!

One word of caution, though: the sounds of machines should be as "right" in feeling as the body movements. It is not enough for the train to go "choo-choo" in two-year-old fashion (unless you have a class of 2-year-olds.) The child should stop and think — what noise does the train really make? Is it an old-fashioned steam engine, or a streamlined diesel? There should be a difference in movement *and* sound.

Since I mentioned trains, here is a list of other forms of transportation to mime:

A brand new sports car	A trolley car
An inflatable dinghy	A sailing ship
A sleek ocean liner	A subway
A helium balloon	A space rocket
A carousel horse	A sled
A skate board	A tractor
An old jalopy	The Concorde
A "Beetle"	A submarine
A dirty old barge	A helicopter

If you wish to build one vast machine, consider the nature of the machine. Here is where research and field trips are especially valuable. If they have the opportunity to visit a real factory, the children will truly appreciate the busy, rhythmic sounds and movement. I divide the children into groups and give each group a different machine. One group made a peanut butter machine, with some children as peanuts, other the crushing part of the machine, while still more became jars, lids, and labels. Other groups might make —

- A complete car wash
- A hot-dog maker
- A paper mill
- A soup canning factory
- A milk-bottling assembly line.

Another Form of Abstract Mime is Working With Feelings

Feelings are not often discussed in our educational system, perhaps because they often don't lend themselves to verbalization. We've all heard children answer

"How was the show?"   "Terrific!"
"What did you do in school today?"   "Nothing."
"Why don't you like it?"   "It's yuccy."

It is not that they do not wish to communicate their innermost feelings, but rather that one handy word suffices, so why use more? Psychiatrists and psychologists have often spent hours trying to elicit a verbal response from an uncommunicative child, when movement, mime, might well have been the key. We often stand helpless when the two-year-old throws himself on the floor, drums his feet into the rug, and expresses his rage through movement. We even respond to *this* with words. "What's the matter, honey? Have you got a pain? You don't like Santa Claus? You don't want Mommy to leave?" All to no avail.

Children, and to a lesser extent adults, express their feelings about the world around them. . .and what is happening inside them. . . through movement.

I usually start with a discussion about feelings. We cannot see them. How do we know they are there? "In what part of your body do you feel?" Most children will reply — "the stomach," though popular idiom would make it the heart. A stomach or a liver is not as romantic on St. Valentine's Day as a pretty red heart!

I begin with feelings children can readily understand. I say, "If I had to take a silent movie of you, could I guess what you are feeling when

. Your dog just got run over;
. You got lost in a big store at Christmas time.
. You are late for school — again!
. Everyone at the party says your outfit looks "weird."
. You try to keep a very big secret at the dinner table.
. You stole a pack of chewing gum from the supermarket.

Covering Up Feelings

When we try to cover up our feelings, the observer has to discern two layers of meaning: first, the facade, the imaginary mask, and second, the true feelings underneath. Here are some exercises where the children can watch one another, and look for these two, or more, layers:

. You want someone to think you are brave. (Really, you are scared stiff.)

. You want everyone to think you are enjoying yourself. (You are not.)

. You want your boss to think you are busy! busy! busy! (You know better.)

. You want someone to think you know what you are doing. (You don't!)

. You want your hostess to think you love her food. (You hate it!)

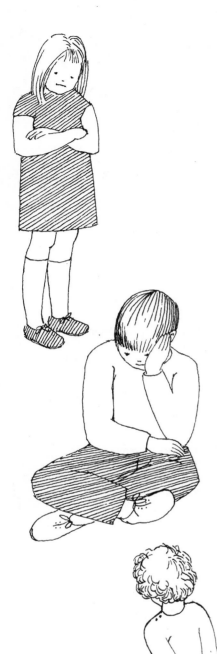

The children are very good at finding their own situations. One boy, doing the last exercise, based his mime on a real-life situation. He had been taken to his grandmother's for dinner. Everyone, except the grandmother, knew she had a month to live. She made all kinds of special Jewish foods for him — he came from a non-Kosher home. Without one word being spoken, he developed many layers of meaning.

Working From the Concrete Feeling to the Abstract

This is not so difficult for children to understand. In medieval morality plays, like *Everyman*, children, as well as adults, watched characters called "Beauty," "Strength," "Death," and "Good Deeds." It was an important part of their instruction, at a time when education was mostly visual: through stained glass windows, statues, pictures, and the movements of the priest at the altar. Perhaps the masked figure of "Death" taught the 15th century child more than today's psychologically—oriented books teach children nowadays.

I ask the children at this point to concentrate more on the feeling (what is happening deep down inside you) and less on who they are and what they are doing. A good introduction to this idea is *Still Pictures, or Statues*. I bring a real camera to class (On one occasion, I brought film too). I say, "I have to take twelve pictures of the way people feel. So when you have really found the feeling, freeze like a statue, and I will take your picture."

The children will enjoy looking at the pictures, and deciding who is the "spirit" of Anger, Boredom, etc.

Bringing The Still Pictures To Life

Now we are ready to unfreeze the statues. Concentrating on that one feeling, how will you move? This exercise is greatly enhanced by music. If you can find someone to play a musical instrument well enough to improvise to the movement, that makes the best possible accompaniment. Otherwise, prepare a tape with mood music. Leave a few seconds blank between the different kinds of music, so that you and the children have a point of transition from one feeling to the next.

I usually start with something

. thoughtful and soft
. hot! hot! hot! hot! hot!
. freezing cold. You are Jack Frost himself, splintering icy cold from top to toe.
. worried. . .the original "worry-wart."
. shy. . .so shy, every part of you says "I'm shy."
. lazy and sleepy. You are not just the laziest person in the world. You are Laziness. "Sloth" is an even better word to describe you.
. greed. You want everything *this* minute!
. Angry. . .fuming. . .furious! You are ready for WAR!
. Peace. . .the spirit of kindness and peace.

Now divide the class into two groups. Play the music for one feeling, let us say "hot," and let the first group all be hot. Suddenly stop the music and bring in the second group. Yes, they are "cold." What will happen when the two groups meet? You can do the same with other contrasting feelings: "War" and "Peace," "Busy" and "Lazy;" "Sad" and "Happy."

Do not be frightened to try these exercises even with very young children. They too need an outlet for strong feelings, and running around the gym or riding a Big Wheel up and down the block is not always the complete answer.

Invite A Response In Movement To Poetry

Poems are written because the poet feels something strongly enough to set it down on paper. I invite the children to look for that initial feeling, the one that made the poet grab his pen and write. How could you show me — through movement — what these poets felt:

MURDER

The house was haunted like spear
My heart was underground
My arms straightened in the fear of death
Everything tumbled in my eyes
Till I felt lead stick in my chest
Till I felt danger
Crushing into my heart

It was the black panther
With dripping spits of fever
Out of his germy mouth
Now no longer I could see the earth
My eyes closed gently
      and slept.

Peter Milosevic, Age 10
Australia*

KINDNESS

A loving arm
Shelters me
From any harm.

The shelteredness
Of kindness
Flows around me.

Mary Flett, age 9
New Zealand

I am a nice nice boy
More than just nice
Two million times more
The word is ADORABLE.

Martin O'Connor, Age 10
New Zealand*

Some stories, too, leave children with a very definite feeling that can be mimed. A beautiful example is "The Giving Tree" by Shel Silverstein (Harper and Row). The focus on this story of the relationship between a tree and a boy is on the feelings of the tree as it goes through all the different stages of "giving."

I prefer not to follow the reading of the poem or story with a lengthy discussion. I like to catch the mood of the moment, let the children respond freely to what the writer suggests. It is exactly the opposite of the analytical, literary approach that many English teachers use. I have no quarrel with them — but mime can be just as "appreciative."

58 Abstract Mime

* From Miracles

Responding To Sounds And Colors And Tastes

Feelings are hard to verbalize; so are sensations. How do you describe a sunset? Today we are bombarded with multiple sensations — we start the day with radio, breakfast, and newspaper, simultaneously. It is hard to "particularize" our response to an individual taste. . .or smell. . .or sound. Mime can help us isolate a sensation and relish it for itself.

I have developed a series of mime lessons based on what we hear, taste, see, smell and touch. I bring in the actual sense stimuli — things to feel, to hear, to taste, to smell. After the children have experienced the sensation, they translate it into movement. Here's a list of the sound effects (from a record) that **prompted one mime lesson**.

. A clanging bell
. Machine guns firing
. A triangle
. Breaking glass
. A horn
. A cry of pain — or a scream
. Rain on a roof
. Prolonged coughing.

Colors, too, can lead to expressive abstract mime. I start this lesson with a discussion on favorite colors (a popular subject with children, I find) and then ask them to show me with their bodies what they feel about different colors. If you have some brightly colored pieces of paper — or fabric — they will add to the honest feelings of this exercise. It is important to stress that everyone feels differently about colors — hence the colors we choose to wear, or to decorate our rooms.

In the middle of one lesson, a child said, "Blind people can't have favorite colors." We concluded that their feelings must be in response to things you could touch. For the next class, we all pretended we were blind, and with eyes tightly closed, felt a variety of (real) fabrics and other materials, and responded to each one in movement. I used velvet. . .a cold slab of marble. . .fur. . .the floor. . .the hair of the child next to you (it was fascinating to watch a white child's response to black curly hair, and the black child's response to long blond hair). . .holly leaves. . .fine soft sand. . . and a sticky lollipop!

I suggested that perhaps sounds could accompany the movements, and the holly shrieked and chirped, while the velvet cooed and hummed.

If you want some terrific movement, try *food* and *drink:*

. Spaghetti
. Meatballs cooking in sauce
. Soda from a soda fountain
. Bread in the oven
. Hamburgers on an outdoor barbecue
. Popcorn — the whole process
. Pretzels
. Eggs being fried.

Tastes and smells can stimulate mime too. *Nosebag Mimes* is a popular game. I bring in some sandwich bags full of smells like pepper and perfume and garlic and mothballs.

As with the previous exercises, the children respond in movement. The children were so interested in watching one another react to nosebags that eventually I had to divide them into groups for "Guess That Smell."

For Older Children — Dreams

If you wish to put all the objects, feelings and sensations into one abstract experience, then the World of Dreams is the obvious choice. If you have ever listened to someone trying to explain in *words* the fantastic dream of the night before, you will understand how inadequate words are. Yet "we are such stuff as dreams are made of," and those of us who experience vivid dreams often want to share them. How many breakfasts are delayed by children anxious to tell their dreams of the night before?

I ask the children to write down everything they remember of a dream the moment they wake up in the morning — and then bring it to class to share with us (a good writing exercise, and one that children enjoy doing). We then act out — in mime — the best of the children's dreams, one after another.

It's also useful to show the children pictures of dreams (such as the dream paintings of Marc Chagall, Hieronymous Bosch, and others). Then we concoct the *Daddy of all Dreams*, one in which everyone takes part.

We started one Big Dream story with a boy tossing and turning in bed. He could *not* get to sleep. "Worries" kept coming in and out of his head. (We used children for "Worries" and they made worry noises.) Finally he took his brain out of his head and put it on the table beside him. At this moment the Worries subsided and the Daddy of all Dreams began, played out to the singing of "Beautiful Dreamer." I suggest you concoct your own dreams, using some of the elements of the fantasies the children give you. It's possible to include totally abstract ideas with no "proper" ending, and the Fantasies can tumble upon one another, as happens in dreams.

At the end an alarm clock rang; the Dreams froze. The boy woke up, put his brain back in his head, the "Worries" started buzzing around, and the morning routine began.

I once did some substitute teaching for several months in a school in England. As I surveyed, with some trepidation, the curriculum I was supposed to teach, my mind turned to mime. It would be a solace for what appeared to be a great deal of stuffy learning. I incorporated mime into practically everything.

Years later, I happened to meet two of my former students, pushing their baby carriages. After the usual exchanges, they both reminisced about how we had "visited Turkey" in mime. They had never forgotten the salient features of the geography of the Near East. As they put it, 'We had been there.''

I would like to give you a few examples of teaching various subjects through mime, and hope that you will find many more yourself! I have not indicated any particular age range because curriculae vary widely, and you can adapt most of the ideas to fit the needs of the children you are working with.

Geography

Apart from Turkey, I have vicariously visited many different lands with my children. Filmstrips, books, television, artifacts can all help to make geography come alive, but mime is firsthand experience, and so makes a greater impact. It makes a "foreign country" seem less "them out there" and more "us," part of the global world. For a city child to mime the harvest of grapes in the vineyards of California makes a "demographic profile" a little more meaningful.

To begin, write down everything you would like the children to remember about that country, in say, ten years' time:

Eskimos: *Climate* (ice, snow, Northern Lights). *Travel* (sea planes, helicopters, sled, ski-doos). *Food* (fishing, seal meat, blubber). *Natural Life* (walrus, polar bears, wolves, sea birds, mostly fish). *Culture* (written, picture language, poetry, song, soapstone carving. *Living* (hunting and fishing.

Develop a story line around any of these factors and you have some exciting mime themes:

"One day a group of Eskimos put on their warm parkas, sipped their hot tea, and ate a meal of whale meat, before crawling out of their igloos and harnessing the dog team. Soon they were speeding across the ice in their sleds in the dark, dark days of winter. It was 11 a.m., but still quite dark. At last they reached the fishing grounds, and just as they were about to take a knife, and cut a hole in the ice, they heard whimpering cries from a nearby ice floe. A baby polar bear had lost its mother! Should they try and rescue the baby? Where was the mother?"

Already you have packed in a good deal of useful geography.

With older children, groups can investigate and mime scenes by themselves, the culminating activity for a social studies unit on any country.

I asked a group of teenagers to show mime scenes which would answer the following questions concerning a country:

1. What is the weather like?
2. Where do you live?
3. What kind of living do you make? Rich? Poor?
4. What is your occupation?
5. How do you travel?
6. What do you eat?
7. What do you wear?
8. How do you use your leisure time?
9. What language do you speak?
10. What are the politics of the country?

I gave each group a map of the country and asked them to close their eyes, and pick a place on the map where their scene would take place. I also encouraged them to find appropriate music as a background for the mime, and any properties that might add color and authenticity.

History

I often ask myself why I was so bored with history in school, and why I love it now. I guess the answer is fairly obvious. I was taught history as a collection of dates and battles, presidents, kings and queens, revolutions and uprisings, and none of it meant very much to me. Yet, now if you flash a date at me, say 1750, a whole host of images rushes to my brain.

I think it is possible for a child to have a similar experience and cultivate an enjoyment for the past. Of course, books, museums, paintings, music and films all will play their part, but mime can be of great importance too, because all battles, all intrigues, all settling of differences, came about through the *movement* of history.

The Boston Tea Party, the making of Pittsburgh, the Battle of Gettysburg, the immigrants arriving at Ellis Island, "building the great railroads," all these moments in history were dramatic movement.

I remember a very energetic, very British lady, wife of an army major, who had taught in army schools all over the world. Emerging from a history lesson, rubbing her hands in glee, she said, "Just done the Battle of Hastings. Desks stacked up, all military strategies worked out with William the Conqueror, Saxons all in battle positions. All troops with swords and shields. Jolly good show!"

Which of those children will ever forget the Battle of Hastings?

Dramatic events in the lives of famous people can make such a character as Julius Caesar, Marco Polo, Daniel Boone or Napoleon come alive.

WHEN HANNIBAL CROSSED THE ALPS

> Hannibal crossed the Alps!
>   Hannibal crossed the Alps!
>   With his black men,
>   His brown men,
>   His countrymen,
>   His town-men,
> With his Gauls, and his Spaniards, his horses and elephants,
> Hannibal crossed the Alps!
>
> Hannibal crossed the Alps!
> Hannibal crossed the Alps!
>   For his bowmen,
>   His spear-men,
>   His front men,
>   His rear men,
> His Gauls and his Spaniards, his horses and elephants,
> Wanted the Roman scalps!
> And *that's* why Hannibal, Hannibal,
> Hannibal crossed the Alps!
>
> *Eleanor Farjeon, from* MIGHTY MEN

I started by reading this poem to a group of children in Watts, L.A. Summer Program. I wanted to work on the life story of a famous Black in history — so I took the bus into downtown L.A. to research Hannibal at the library. When I came back to Watts with the whole story of this great general who had lived from 247 to 183 B.C., the children were fascinated. Apart from the historically famous "Crossing the Alps," Hannibal commanded fifteen other major battles, and never lost one. When he was finally taken prisoner by the Romans, he took poison (which he kept in a secret hiding place in a ring he wore on his finger) rather than live under Roman rule.

If we were going to cross the Alps, we needed to go into the geography of these mighty mountains. So we plotted Hannibal's route on a map. Now we needed "Gauls, Spaniards, horses, elephants, bowmen and spearmen." How would an elephant respond to the ice and snow of the Alps? First we had to become the elephant, and then climb the mountains. We had to practice the use of 2nd century B.C. spear, shield and bow. Now we had to shape a life history into a story climaxing in the dramatic death of

Hannibal himself. They boy who played "my" Hannibal made the most of the occasion. The Roman soldiers were just about to descend upon him, when Hannibal looked all around him, then at his ring; he bit the top off the ring, spat it on the floor, and then swallowed the poison, just as the Roman spears were upon him.

Nearly everyone in the group wanted to play Hannibal, including one girl, so we acted out the story several times, with a different Hannibal taking the lead each time we did it.

Language Arts

Start with the alphabet warm-up exercise from Chapter II (page 11). Now develop the exercise into vocabulary building, spelling lists, and the use of phonetic sounds. Introduce body masks made out of large cards with different letters of the alphabet printed on them. Half the class will make up words with their body masks, and the other half will mime the words.

Mime synonyms and antonyms from the weekly spelling lists:

1) First child mimes the word
2) Second child mimes the synonym of that word
3) Third child mimes the antonym

One child gives directions in mime: "Come here!" Turn around," "Follow me," "Stop!" "Go away," "Keep quiet," "Hurry," "Hooray!" The rest of the class write down the words he is miming.

Occupational Mime from Cards

Send round a box, and let each child pick a card, read it, turn the card face down, and mime the action. Funny tasks like these are good for mime as well as reading comprehension:

1) You have bubble gum stuck to your teeth. Try and get it off.

2) There is a huge plate of spaghetti in front of you. You are so hungry, but you have no fork.

3) You have glued your feet together by mistake.

4) You are a short-sighted tight-rope walker who has lost his glasses.

5) Your shoes are full of sand. Clean them out.

6) You are eating a candy and you do not like it. Try and take it out, so no one will see you.

7) Wash your hair, and just as you are dripping with soap, the water is turned off.

8) Pretend you are your mother, who has not made your bed in two weeks. What will she find?

The same thing can be done on a simpler level with jobs, written on cards and then mimed for the rest of the class to guess what you are doing: Mailmen, garbage collector, cook, dentist, hairdresser, carpenter, teacher, plumber, tailor, auto mechanic.

Verbal Dynamics

Verbal dynamics is something that I have used in teaching many different subjects — but I think its best application is through oral language development.

Many of the words in the English language have an onomatopoeic quality which can be very dynamic. You taste and enjoy, and roll the words around your mouth. A

Name: Caroline

young child, just learning to talk understands and delights in both the sound *and* the movement of words: "Poke! Poke! Poke!" he will go, delighting in the explosive "P" and the hard "K," and the fun of the poking movement with his finger.

In this exercise, we go back to that original feeling for words, through movement. Start with verbs (the *doing* words):

spring	bend	lift
drag	pull	push
peek	stride	press

Now mime the action of "spring" while speaking the word "spring," synchronizing the two exactly. Begin word and movement at exactly the same moment. You will be surprised at the good sounds you are hearing!

This exercise is not confined to verbs. You can use it with almost any word in the language. I once asked a group of children to write down a list of words, gathered from the sign and billboards they passed on the highway during a class trip. I asked another group to bring the five words they remembered best from a TV commercial. We then used these exotic lists with the same kind of emphasis the advertisers had originally intended, except we did it through movement and sound.

If you would like to work on proper nouns, then **names and nicknames** are a good idea. Many children have a name on their birth certificate which makes them feel one way, whereas the nickname is the "real child."

Verbal dynamics is particularly helpful in teaching good expressive reading. So often children only stress the adjectives, or read in a monotone. If you have a session in verbal dynamics, and then pick up the reading books, and apply the same kind of enjoyment to the printed page, your readers will sound much more interesting.

If you like to do choral reading with your children, try "moving the words" first. If you look at the poem, "Hannibal Crossed the Alps" and you mime such words as "black," "elephants," "spear-men," "scalps," first, and *then* read the poem, chorally, you should have something more than a dull, meaningless, song-song delivery.

One final word on verbal dynamics. It works much better with a group that has some experience in mime and movement. Others feel too inhibited. Even quite young children will "forget" to do words and movement together, unless they have some experience in mime, so the whole point of the exercise is lost.

Creative Writing

This is such an obvious extension of a mime lesson. To write from first hand, from the gut of your experience, is surely what we mean by creative writing. Every part of mime lends itself to the written word, both poetry and story writing. With many projects you may want to leave the mime scene unfinished, so that the children can sit down and write their own endings.

There is something particularly satisfying about writing immediately after a great deal of physical action. Robert Frost said, "The most important thing in writing poetry is the application of the seat of the pants to the seat of the chair", and then he might have added, "having something to write about." If they are used to the story-making process through mime, they can more readily translate this to the written word.

Sometime children are stimulated by mime and masks to write a play. You will see a play written for monster masks by a seven-year old in Chapter 10.

Nickname: Coco

After character work you might ask: "Write me a play that brings in all characters we have been working on, perhaps, a fairy tale, perhaps a scary tale, perhaps a funny tale."

or —

"Listen to this music. Remember the story we mimed when we were all lost in the desert? We could never find a really good ending. Write one."

I once taught a mime lesson all about hands. The children had just come from gym, so they needed to sit quietly in their desks. We started by looking at our own hands. What did they tell us about ourselves?

"If you bite your nails, you're nervous." "If you have warts and cuts and broken nails, you like gardening, or fixing things." "If your hands are smooth and very clean, perhaps you are smooth and clean."

Now I asked the children to show me different feelings, just using their hands, as though I was taking a close-up picture with a 200 mm. lens on the camera

"Show me hands that are: shy,
                              cruel,
                              bored,
                              happy.

Let the camera zoom in on the hands of different characters. With some of these people, rings, gloves, watches, and bracelets will tell us who they are, as well as the movements they make.

I then showed the children a book of poetry and photographs, "The Wonder of Hands" by Edith Baer (published by Parents Magazine Press).

By now, the children had plenty of ideas for writing poems about what hands can do, and the results were very original.

Math

One famous method of teaching mathematics in the elementary school, is through the use of cuisinaire rods. To do this, a teacher needs a complete kit of all the different colored rods. A friend of mine, an elementary school teacher, was annoyed one day when another teacher was using her cuisinaire equipment just when she had planned to use it. I suggested she substitute human rods, with colored masks, using the children themselves as "the kit." Both teacher and "kit" produced excellent results.

A good lesson for kindergartners is based on *shapes*. One way to do this is to use masking tape and make four different shapes on the floor. . .square, triangle, rectangle and circle. Have the children sit on the shape and then think about its qualities. "What is 'square' to you?" The children can take turns to respond individually or in pairs to what the shape means to them. This project can be taken realistically, or in an abstract manner.

Circus Numbers

An interesting math game at grade 1 level developed from circus mimes. The children had been working for several weeks on their own circus, and when it was over, they were reluctant to abandon this successful theme. So a teacher-friend decided to incorporate this knowledge into her math class.

All the children stand in a circle like circus horses. Each child is given a card to hang around their neck with a different number on it (from 1 to 20). When the circus music starts, the horses prance around the circle until it stops. The ringmaster (you — or a child), hits the floor with a stick, the horses stand tall, and the teacher calls out an equation. The horse (child) who has the answer on the card, must come into the center of the ring, and stamp out the correct answer, like a horse, with his feet. The music starts again, and the procedure is repeated until every child has had a turn.

Music Appreciation

Throughout this book, there have been constant allusions to music and mime, and by the time you have finished with any course on mime, you are bound to have moved to a lot of music. Music appreciation is part of mime, in a very natural way. We have become so used to music as a background to other parts of our life that it is important to provide a place where the child can actively respond, listen with his whole body to music. I remember a teenager who told me he hated classical music ("that garbage"), who responded marvelously to Prokofiev's music when played as a background to a mime on "dying in the desert."

Art

I have often received unsolicited drawings and paintings following a mime lesson. You may want to ask the children to draw or paint what they have done in mime straight after the lesson. If you are working with the art teacher, apart from making masks, you might find you have other areas in common. If you are working on abstract ideas in mime, as suggested in the previous chapter, this can tie in with the art teacher's lesson on abstract art. Invite the art teacher to watch a particularly graphic lesson. She may have as many ideas for you as you have for her.

Aspects Of Learning Outside The Curriculum

Let us suppose that, as a teacher, you are concerned about

· Animal rights	· Violence
· Smoking	· Discrimination
· Gun control	· World hunger

Mime is a very good way to get your message across. It may succeed where countless posters and pamphlets, lectures and sermons have failed.

In the late 1950's, in Europe, there were still thousands of refugees left in camps after the war, living wretched existences in a stateless society. I was very concerned. We started with a choral reading of W.H. Auden's poem, "Refugee Blues," and then, to some poignant blues music, we developed a story — in mime — of the fate of a refugee family. Was it didactic? Of course. . .but, for both the teenagers who enacted the mime, and the audience who watched it, it was a moving experience.

Here is just one treatment on the issue of *Smoking*. Show, in mime, the progression of smoke through the human body and its effects after several years of heavy smoking. Half the class will become different parts of the body: the nose, mouth, teeth, throat, lungs, hands. The other half, dressed in black and wearing skeleton-like masks, will be the cigarette smoke. This is most effective with sound effects of breathing and coughing. The mime can be repeated at different intervals in the life of the cigarette smoker's body:

- · Age 16 — one pack a day
- · Age 20 — 2 packs a day
- · Age 40 — 3 packs a day. Finish as you wish!

I first started to work with children and masks, after visiting a school where the art teacher had made, and put on display in the corridor, a collection of beautiful and exciting masks. They had painted eyes, so I knew that they were ornaments, but as I looked at these colorful, primitive, strange faces, they seemed to be saying, "Take us down off the shelf, make us move, give us life."

I felt like the famous clown, Grock, who said, "Ever since I can remember, all kinds of inanimate objects have had a way of looking at me reproachfully, and whispering to me in unguarded moments: we've been waiting for you. At last you've come. . . take us now and turn us into something different. . .we've been so bored waiting."

What would happen, I wondered, if we took down this set of false faces, and let the children try them out? What could be done with them? I had used masks myself, in my own drama training — but could this approach be applied to children. At first, I experimented with a teenage class — with spectacular results. Now, in my work with student teachers, I regularly introduce masks, about a third of the way through the course. It is usually the highlight of the course, and often the turning point for many students.

The Face For Special Occasions

Those that have felt a little shy, or uncertain, given the opportunity to hide behind a new and different face, suddenly develop great freedom of expression. It is quite uncanny. The mask works its magic every time. It is as if the timid person is saying, "It doesn't matter now what I do, because it isn't really me doing it — it's the mask." With a new face comes a new personality. We all know, and recognize, that it is the face that makes the greatest difference between you and me. When you confront a new group of students, the first thing you will notice will be their faces. Carl Sandburg says,

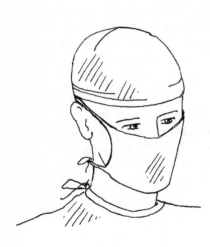

> This face you got, this here phizzog you carry around,
> Somebody shipped it to you, and it was like a package marked:
> No goods exchanged after being taken away.
> This face you got.

While this may be true for everyday life, from Stone Age times to present day, for *special occasions,* we human beings have always needed a special face. We all need the time and the occasion to "prepare a face to meet the faces that you meet." Even without the physical, actual mask, all of us put on a special face from time to time: when we go to a place of worship, or job interview, or funeral home. Children are taught to say "cheese" for the camera; "Look happy, it's your birthday," "Watch out, the principal's coming." One of the enduring delights of "Candid Camera" is the fact that the TV camera catches people without their "special-for-TV-faces."

The ancient Egyptians, the Indians, and many other civilizations believed that the mask was necessary to confront their gods. . .or to scare away devils and evil spirits. The robber and the lady wearing a yashnak are hiding from the world. The motor cyclist and the surgeon use the mask for protection. The clown and the "trick-or-treater" want to change personality and to have fun. The masked participants in a Mardi-Gras procession are using the mask for a special tradition.

The Mask In Drama

Our western dramatic tradition may be said to have started with the mask. In ancient Greece, Thespis extracted a leader from his group of choral dancers, and gave him a collection of masks to wear. Thespis was not ready for the interplay between different characters, playing different roles, but he did understand that false faces, worn by a single actor, could make "theatre."

The mask was worn on stage for the next few hundred years, all through the great dramas of the Greek theatre, and on through the comedies of the Roman mimes. When we pick up the tradition again, in medieval times, we find the plays to be mostly religious and the masks used to portray evil characters like devils. With the coming of the Renaissance, and the elevation of the spoken word, masks were taken over by the true professionals — the Commedia dell' Arte players.

And I have only considered the Western tradition. All over the world, in theatre and dance, in religion and art, the mask has played a prominent part.

Using Masks Today

The mask and the puppet have walked hand in hand (or should I say, "hand and face"?) throughout history. Today puppets are alive and well, and flourishing in theatre

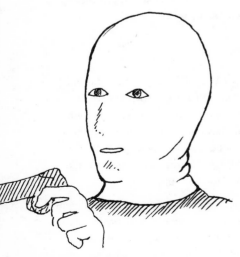

69 Introduction to Masks

and education. Go to your local library — you will find the shelves filled with books on how to make puppets, and how to use them. There is hardly a child in America who has not had the pleasure of turning his/her hand into some kind of puppet character.

The same cannot be said of masks. We are in danger of losing a very vital and viable form of expression. As "civilization" takes its toll on the few remaining "primitive" peoples of our world, so the wonderfully carved, beautiful masks are rejected in favor of TV sets and motorcycles. Well-meaning Western art collectors may gather the masks, and swoop them off to museums, where they will be put into glass cases, labelled, and looked upon, but never, ever again will the dynamic witch doctor or the thankful warrior pound the earth, wearing the mask, putting it to use, dancing, moving — making the mask live, and speak.

In our mime work we can bring back that tradition. One of the main reasons I use masks with children is because I know how much they like to guess. For a baby, less than a year old, the best game of all is peek-a-boo. "Now I see your face — now I hide it — here it comes again!" . . .the oldest, the best game in the world to a baby. The mask is another kind of "peek-a-boo."

The Mummenshanz players, the very popular masked mime players who appeared on Broadway and television, draw their names from the Swiss medieval tradition of wearing masks while playing games ("mummen") of chance ("shantz"). For them, the mask is the original poker face. Put it on, and your opponent cannot guess, by the light in your eyes or slightly upturned mouth, that you hold the trump. Walter Kerr says, "Why a poker face on stage? To keep the sharp-eyed guessing. Children like to be kept guessing." And indeed they do, Mr. Kerr.

Children also need to wear a different face, when they just cannot stand "the old phizzog someone shipped them." While trying on someone else, through the mask, the child learns more about himself. He feels free to be anyone or anything. The mask works a magic spell; puts him in touch with some inner creative sparks, and sends them flying out into the world.

But masks are not something to be used for every mime class. They should keep their "special occasion" quality — and come as the climax to your work in mime. Often I suggest activities that will lead up to that big moment when you put on the mask. Also I have used the term "mask" loosely to include make-up and extra appendages like beards and moustaches that give the child a new face in other ways.

Now To A Few Practical Considerations

When should you start mask work? Almost any age. After all, it is the two-year-old who enjoys peek-a-boo and clowning around the most. With *very* little children, a collection of (soft) old hats, some with eyes already cut out, are just perfect for trying on and dancing around. Every nursery school should have such a box. Go to rummage sales and pick up all the old hats. Play lots of peek-a-boo, and see who can be the funniest. . .who can be the scariest. . .who looks like the janitor, and who looks like Santa Claus. Very simple. . .but more fun than ordinary dress-up.

From kindergarten onwards, you can start using masks made from a variety of different materials. Paper is probably the most popular — paper bags, paper plates, **papier-mache,** origami (the Japanese art of folded paper), cardboard, boxes, egg cartons, and so on. But you will also need scarves. . .cloths. . .scraps of material. . .yarn. . .feathers. . . almost any kind of junk.

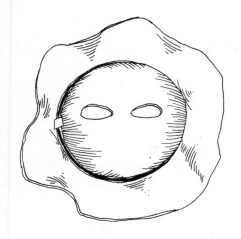

The Aztecs made masks of stone; in Siam, gold masks were placed on the faces of the dead; in India, they made masks out of bronze; the Arabs used animal skins, while the Iroquois Indians created corn husk masks. My own experience is that *anything* can be made into a mask. A boy I knew, whose father was a bus driver, made a beautiful bird mask using different colored bus transfers for the feathers! A friend of mine wove a mask out of straw, string, yarn, and odd scraps of material. My two-year-old (I admit he is mask-minded) took a green tray from the vegetables we bought in the supermarket, made two holes for eyes, and used it as a mask.

Comfort And Safety

Whenever you are wearing a mask, you must consider the comfort and safety of the wearer. All children know you must *never* put a plastic bag over your face — but suffocation could occur with other materials. Always check for breathing.

If you are a kindergarten teacher with twenty children you will not want to make paper plate masks which have to be tied with string behind twenty heads — unless you are practicing bow tying! In fact, almost any method is better than the string at the back of the head. I avoid strings whenever possible.

If you are not artistically inclined, and you are asking an art teacher or friend to make the masks for you, let me give you a word of caution, from my own experience. The first time I asked an art teacher to make masks for me, she was thrilled to bits. She made the most gorgeous masks. However, they were so uncomfortable we could not use them. Many artistic minds, it seems, do not think in terms of seeing through the mask, wearing it energetically, or even slipping on the new face with ease. Most art is a static business — but the masked Mime uses his body as his chief material. Remind the art teacher to try the mask on, and move in it.

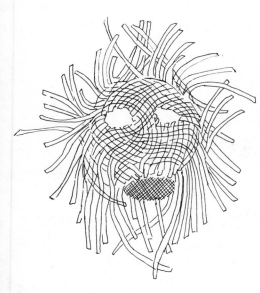

If the masks are to be used regularly — perhaps in a performance — they should be made of something fairly durable, or they can easily fall apart at a crucial moment. The most durable mask is probably papier-mache or cloth, stuffed and shaped and decorated as you wish.

What Kind Of Space Will You Be Working In?

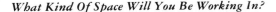

If you will be using the platform-style stage (proscenium arch), you might like to make frontal masks. By this, I mean the kind of mask, like a paper plate, that is really only interesting from the front. Even sideways, the dramatic effect is lost. I hate to say to any child, "Don't turn your back to the audience." But, for certain kinds of mask, the old maxim is unfortunately true. On the plus side, have you ever felt that all those grey (black, green) curtains that surround the average school stage were mostly just a big nuisance? Here, at last, with masks, they will come into their own. After all, for all good peek-a-boo, you have to have some place to hide. . .and then jump out!

If you are working in a classroom, make good use of it. Use blackboards and closets to hide behind, doors with glass windows for masked faces to peek through, and have a group of "scaredy-cats" hide beneath desks.

The same principles apply to large halls and gyms. Use what is available. Some of my best mask work was done in a basement room which had a huge shelf running down one wall. I shall never forget three masked witches scuttling along that shelf, making strange incantations. If you happen to be out-of-doors, then your masked figures can leap out from behind bushes and trees, barns, and rocks.

If you are lucky enough to have video-tape equipment, then here is its ideal use. Even people who hate to see themselves on TV can never object when wearing a mask! Many children move best of all when wearing a mask. If this good dynamic movement can be captured on film, it can be a very positive experience. "Is that *really* me, doing all those crazy things?" they ask, happily incredulous.

Special Effects To Add

Music and sound effects — as well as narrative — can all play an important part in your work with masks. In the following chapters I give ideas for suitable music or "utterance" — that is, sounds the mask wearers make themselves. I've also suggested sound effects for you and the other children to provide with drums, cymbals, triangles, sticks, woodblocks, and wind instruments, like recorders and flutes.

A tape recorder, with the selected pieces all pre-recorded, is usually easier to operate than a record player. I ruined a beautiful recording of Sibelius' Second Symphony, while rehearsing a mime to the story of Prometheus. When it came to the actual performance, we had to buy a new record.

Is Mime the Only Art Form to be Used with a Mask?

Certainly not — the mask began with the dance, and is still used in ballet, modern dance, and the folk dances of many different lands. How about scripted plays with masks? There are a few, written during this century. Eugene O'Neil used masks in *The Great God Brown,* and *All God's Chillin Got Wings.* Andre Obey's beautiful play *Noah,* uses masked animals, and W.B. Yeats wrote four poetic dance dramas, expecially for use with masks. In theatre for children, where the characterization is broader, more fantastical, we are more likely to meet animal or bird masks, clowns, witches, and even stranger creatures. In Maeterlinck's play *The Bluebird*, there is a part for a "Loaf of Bread" (a lovely character to play in a body mask). In *Theseus and the Minotaur,* the costumer has to make a minotaur — no mean undertaking! In *Alice in Wonderland*, there are dormice and white rabbits, mad hatters and packs of cards. *Beauty and the Beast* requires an ugly masked creature with a handsome young man underneath — and so we could go on.

I would like you, ultimately, to use masks in many different ways — and the culmination of all work on mime and masks might be a play. Most work with masks is movement, and often it is difficult to see and speak through the most comfortable of masks - so - start with mime, and enjoy your masks for their great visual effect. If you want a good project that does use words — ask the children to write plays for masks, but only when they have "been there" — worn the magic mask for themselves. You should find some very creative writing.

The Greeks used masks, originally, to change characters. The new face (mask) had to be immediately, recognizably, different from the one that went before. Their masks were *not* neutral.

Yet that is exactly what a mask can be: neutral. There is one mask — plain white, large enough to be molded to the contours of any face — that presents an almost blank face to the world. It is devoid of any special nose or mouth, with just holes for eyes. It may say anything, be anyone, acquire many different moods. It all depends on the face and body beneath the mask. One person may wear it, and it looks old and sad; another puts it on, and suddenly, with his quick movements and upright posture, the mask looks young and happy. Turn the mask very slowly. . .up right, down left. . . the feelings are different again. I cannot give any scientific explanation for this strange occurance — so it just must be magic. In fact, this faceless face is the most magical of all masks.

The best neutral mask is made of papier-mache. In making it, always think center, making two identical halves. Asymmetrical masks may be interesting, but they are certainly not neutral.

Ideally, everyone should have his or her own neutral papier-mache mask, but you can work with simple white paper masks, or even share a single neutral mask.

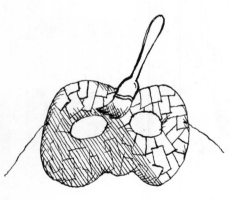

Activities To Begin Work With A Neutral Mask

Put on the mask yourself, and without "acting" — that is, without projecting any particular character or mood, sit in a chair. Look about you. . .look into the distance. . . study something close up. . .pick up a book and read. . .move about the room, examining different objects, searching for something.

Now ask the children for their reactions. You will be surprised! I guarantee the mask said much more than you did! Now let someone else repeat the same simple movements, wearing the mask. Choose a child, perhaps of the opposite sex, with a body shape and temperament very different from your own. I think you will find the answers to such questions as "Who is he?" "What does he feel?" or "How old is he?" quite different. Let the next neutral mask wearer respond to a piece of music with a very definite mood. Now switch masks with a new child and a new piece of music. Then go back and play the first piece of music with yet another masked Mime.

You may want to add sound effects, made by the rest of the group: humming, hissing, clicking the tongue against the roof of the mouth, a "wolf" whistle, tapping, heavy breathing, wind sounds, a series of crashes or creaks.

One thing becomes obvious with any mask work: the interest is in the eye of the beholder. Often the mask wearer is not even completely aware of how effective his or her movement may be. Students will soon realize, through watching one another, that their movements must be larger than life. Without reliance on the face as the main means of expression, the feelings have to be shown through other parts of the body. The audience, watching, suddenly becomes aware of interesting feet, or hunched up shoulders, or the tilt of the entire masked head.

Here is a list of simple basic actions I suggest to the children for use with the neutral mask. If everyone has a mask, everyone may do them together, but if you have only a few masks, remember that in mask work the audience interest is somehow higher than with regular mime.

. Search for something that is lost.

. Wait for someone who is late.

. Listen, with growing anxiety, for someone who is following you. Eventually find somewhere to hide.

. Explore a haunted house at midnight.

. Study a very large picture carefully, trying to decide if you will buy it.

. Wait, as a spy, to pounce!

. Try to avoid being noticed looking through the sale rack in the cheapest clothing store in town.

. Discover that you can suddenly see, after being blind all your life. . .or the other way round.

. Get out of a cage by bending the bars with your bare hands. But first, you have to untie your hands, somehow — and then your feet.

An interesting exercise is to divide the class into two groups. One group watches; the other group performs. Now divide the performing group into two. Half wear neutral masks, and the other half wear no masks. Use any of the mime exercises you have used earlier; you will be surprised to see how the use of the mask changes the exercise. Here are some mimes that are effective:

74 Character Masks

. Ride on a crowded elevator. . .subway. . .street.
. Pick your way through a garbage-strewn, puddly street.
. Wait on a street corner in a "dangerous" part of town.
. Pace the office floor, thinking through a difficult letter.
. Work with computers and machines.
. Search for books in the library.
. Watch an important game on television in a store window.

Now the audience group has a turn to perform, and the others can watch. There are many comparisons you can make between those who wore the mask and those who did not.

You may find the neutral mask interesting to work with in conjunction with other types of mask — say, in the middle of a group of colorful monster masks. Or introduce it (it's definitely an "it!") into work with more specific and definite characters. Having worked with this very special mask, do not put it on a shelf and forget about it. It has so much to say.

A Scarf Is Another Kind Of Neutral Mask

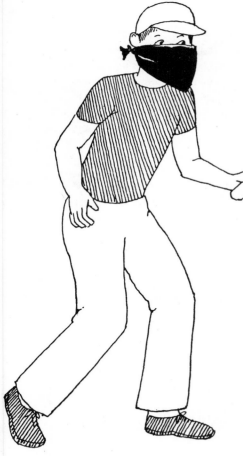

You can use just an ordinary head scarf. I ask the children to borrow an old one from their mothers and bring it to mime class. I begin by saying, "Put on your scarves. Who do you feel like?"

Most children adopt the traditional way of wearing the scarf. . .like a peasant (I always feel like a Russian peasant in a headscarf!) Here are some of the answers children have given me:

A robber	A gypsy
Little Red Riding Hood	A witch
An old lady	"I'm going to church"
A pirate	A cowboy

Somebody on a wet and windy day who just had her hair done

I like to act out these different characters in a variety of situations. If we take the character of the robber. . .children really feel like a robber with the scarf tied around the face. Put on some stealthy "music-to-rob-by" (we have used "Hernando's Hide-away" from *Pajama Game*) and set up all kinds of imaginary staircases to climb, windows to squeeze through, ledges to creep along, corridors to sneak down, doors to hide behind, difficult safe combinations to crack; and passing police cars.

Nancy Pereira, in her book *Creative Dramatics in the Library,* gives many excellent ideas for the use of cloths (square pieces of material, very much like my headscarf). The children take the cloth (or headscarf), and turn it into

. Dracula's cape as he steals back to his coffin in the dead of night
. A bullfighter's cloak. Ole!
. A magician's handkerchief
. A blanket to wrap around a newborn baby
. A bridal veil
. A weight lifter's muscle (roll the scarf in a ball and put it up your sleeve)
. A towel for a swimmer just out of the ocean on a not-too-warm day
. The napkin worn by a waiter in a fancy restaurant.

This is an excellent introduction to mask work. Now ask the children to cover their faces completely. It is best if the scarf hangs down freely. If you are concerned about it falling off, then tie two corners of the scarf loosely at the back of the neck. This gives much the same effect as the neutral mask. The best kind of scarf to use is made of chiffon, or some other see-through material.

Any of the exercises for the neutral mask work well with scarves. You can also ask the class to express feelings. . .anger. . .shame. . .grief. . .joy. . .boredom. . . greed. . .dreaminess. . .surprise. . .sulkiness. Here are a few other ideas, with no specific characterization involved:

. "Hello" in as many different ways as you can
. "Good-bye" in as many different ways as you can
. "Locked in!" Escape from a trunk, a garbage can, a well, a dark room, a fortune cookie, a whale.
. "Locked out!" of your home, your car, a place with huge doors, a beautiful garden with high walls (as in the story, *The Selfish Giant*, by Oscar Wilde).
. "Help!"
. "I'm gonna tell your mother!"
. "I wish, I wish. . ." What do you wish?
. "Oh, no, you don't". . .Do what?
. "Maybe just one more." One more what?

By now you will have evidence that mask work is different from mime without masks. Movements have to be much bigger, often with broad, sweeping gestures. It's a larger statement. Let me give you an example. If I ask an unmasked mime class to show me "Fear," I might expect the kind of expression on the left. The child relies on the face as the principal means of expression. Now, if we put on a mask, we are more likely to find the reaction on the right.

If the gesture seems vaguely familiar to you, it is because you have seen it adorning frescoes and vases, showing the Greek actors using the traditional gesture for "Fear."

Changing Character Through Masks

Our original Greek dramatist, Thespis, would not have been satisfied with the neutral mask. With it, the face behind is in charge of the personality. In most instances, the neutral mask is just a further extension of our own personalities; thus, I was not surprised that a difficult, hyper-active sixth grader made his neutral mask into a tense, uneasy character, while a plump, relaxed little girl fell easily into the role of a funny old lady with her neutral mask.

But the purpose of the Greek mask was to change character, from one face into something else very definite, and different. Theatre in ancient Greece took place out of doors, in bright sunlight with the brilliant blue of the Mediterranean Sea, stark against the rugged hills and rocks. A masked figure had to be seen, and recognized immediately. No time for the subtleties of the neutral mask and the interplay of softened, artificial light. Here and now, from the back of the theatre (the top of the hillside), we must see, and feel, the presence of the hero-King, or the old blind messenger, or the Cyclops. With these strongly masked characters, the mask itself will tell you how it wants you to behave. It's the boss! In the Cyclops mask, there is no way you can become a funny old lady. You are a giant, so you need *big* movements, and you look out at the world from your one huge eye.

Paper-Plate Masks

To begin character work in masks, try paper plates . . . regular white paper plates, and use magic markers, paint, "M & M" candies for eyes, wool, masking tape, tissue paper, paper decals, fabric, anything else you can think of to help make a particular character.

How do you feel today? Sad, sleepy, lonely, shy, naughty, pretty, silly, surprised, half-sad, half-happy, sneaky, cute, hopeful, mean. Base your character mask on one of these feelings. Even four-year-olds can appreciate this work. Paper plate masks work well glued to a fat popsicle stick. Then they become hand masks, held in front of the face, like a fan.

Here is a "peek-a-boo" guessing game with paper plate masks, for small children. Seat the children in a circle, and place the masks face down on the floor. As each child puts on the mask and shows the character through movement, we all sing this little song:

> Who is behind the false face?
> Nobody knows but me
> I won't tell you —
> You will have to guess.
> If you guess right — (name the child)
> I will answer "yes."

I encourage discussion about the character of each mask, and ask the child to find an appropriate name for their mask. In the manner of 17th century Restoration plays, the name (Lady Squeamish, Sir Jasper Fidget, Colonel Bully) suits the character.

I have had some interesting discussions about the discovery that, "Today I don't feel the same way I did when I made the mask." Feelings change. What do we do? We have to act. . .pretend. Do the people we see on television really feel that way? Is the puppeteer who operates Oscar the Grouch really grouchy when he's not on TV? I once had a pretty deep discussion on Method Acting with a group of kindergarten children, all starting with paper plate masks.

Let us now introduce Silly Sally and Naughty Norman in a proper fashion. I set up a "Celebrity Corner" in the classroom and, in the manner of the televised talk shows, I introduce each masked character. If you happen to have a piano — and Carmino Ravosa's *Piano Sound Effects* music, you can play appropriate entrance music for each character. The masked characters enter from behind a door, curtain, blackboard or closet, and then walk and sit, according to character. You may want to interview this interesting group of people and introduce them to one another. What will happen when Sad Sue meets Happy Harry? Could they possibly exchange masks, and see what it feels like to be someone different? Lonely Lisa met Lonesome Laurie, and they became such good friends that they threw away their masks and hugged one another.

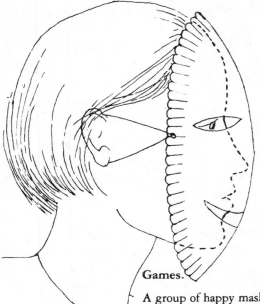

With older children, there are some other useful exercises with character masks, based on the effects our feelings have on the rest of the world. This can still be done with paper plate masks, but you will need both hands free, so punch holes through the side of the mask, close to the ears. Bend the tips of two pipe cleaners into hooks and attach them through the holes. Bend the other ends of the pipe cleaners round the ears, like eyeglasses. You can do the same thing, threading rubber bands through the holes, and then hooking them over the ears. Another method is to tie string at the back of the head. Make sure it is thick string, or you will find yourself tied to that character forever — unless you cut the strings!

Games.

A group of happy masks is having a wonderful time playing games (baseball, bingo, snowballs, marbles). Suddenly a very different kind of character comes in wearing a mask that is Sad, Mean, Angry — a contrast. The focus of the group is entirely changed from the happy concentration on the game to an interchange between characters. I usually let the children find their own ending. One group became so infuriated with the intruder — and each other — that they needed double-faced masks. At the end of the game they flipped over the masks to reveal Mad faces.

Beggars.

A group of rich, spoiled people, in masks, are all greedily enjoying a sumptuous meal. Suddenly they are invaded by a group of starving beggars.

Big Boss.

The Boss mask marches in with all her underlings (perhaps Silly Sue, Lazy Louis, and Scaredy-Cat Cathy). There is a big job to be done, like painting a room, setting up a camp, or building a house. Nobody will cooperate. (Many of the funniest comedy routines of the silent movies are based on this type of situation.)

Parade.

A mixed group of characters — some bored, some fussy, some excited — are waiting for the parade to go by. At last, we hear parade music in the distance. It grows louder, and a whole parade of masked characters goes by:

  . soldiers
  . Girl Scouts
  . The most important person in the parade
  . clowns
  . beauty queens
  . V.I.P.'s

The Old Person.

The character, who lives all alone, wears an old, sad mask. One morning he/she wakes up, and realizes that it is his/her birthday. He putters around the kitchen, making coffee and feeling sad. He goes to the mailbox . No mail. He sits down with his coffee and slowly drops off to sleep. Suddenly there is a knock on the door. The old person wakes up and opens the door to find four masked characters bearing gifts —

  . "Happy" bringing a birthday cake
  . "Patience" with a handknit sweater
  . "Beauty" bringing flowers
  . "Kindness" bringing a puzzle or game.

The music of "Happy Birthday" strikes up and plays continuously throughout the dream sequence. They exchange greetings, arrange the flowers in a vase, try on the sweater, cut and eat the birthday cake. Now everyone settles down to try the puzzle. Suddenly the "Happy Birthday" music stops. The guests have to leave. Before they go, they persuade the old person to take off the "sad" mask. Very shyly and slowly he does. Then he waves good-bye, hugs the warm sweater to himself, admires the flowers, eats one more *small* piece of cake, and continues with the puzzle as he falls asleep. When he wakes up, the cake, the sweater, the flowers have all gone. Sadly, the old person reaches for the mask and puts it back on.

All the properties in this are mimed, so I suggest you do it with children who have worked on occupational mime.

Sharp!

A mime for four characters — Sharp Eyes, Sharp Nose, Sharp Ears, Sharp Tongue. The masks should accentuate the particular features of each character. Half-masks here offer the greatest freedom of movement. In the frontispiece to this chapter, you will notice that Sharp Tongue is a mask for the lower half of the face, offering the great advantage of leaving the eyes completely free. The Sharp Quartet may embark on great adventures: espionage in a foreign country; beach-combing for buried treasure, or making their way through the Carnival without a dime to spend.

The Seven Dwarfs.

Each in a different mask showing the character that goes with their name — Dopey. . . Doc. . .Happy. . .Sneezy. . .Grumpy. . .Bashful. . .Sleepy — the Seven Dwarfs are busy in the mine until it's time to go home for dinner. They are delighted to find Snow White (no mask) and the supper on the table, the house clean, etc. You can continue with the story, bringing in the Wicked Queen, if you wish, disguised in the mask of an old apple-seller.

Peanuts.

One of the reasons this gang has been so successful is because the characters are very basic and simple. Children can identify with them. Many of the Charlie Brown books are very actable. Masks can be simple: draw a picture of the Peanuts character's face and paste it onto the cut-off top of a paper bag mask. Around Halloween, the story of Snoopy hiding behind a pumpkin in the big Pumpkin Patch is fun to do.

Walt Disney.

These could be made in the same way as the Peanuts' masks, using the faces of the Walt Disney characters. The Walt Disney book *Storyland* has many good stories to act — The Sorcerer's Apprentice; Dumbo; Donald Duck; Private Eye; Micky Mouse and Pluto Pup, etc. All the characters are lovable and fun for younger children to play. I consider this character work rather than animal mime because these characters are known more for their human characteristics than their true animal quality.

All the above character masks could be made with paper plates, papier-mache, or folded paper. Do remember that most of these masks are more interesting to the audience from the front. The children should try not to turn their backs to the audience.
It helps to watch your own character mask in action — on someone else — to get a better understanding of what the mask is telling you to do and what effect it will have on an audience. If you have a stage, let each masked character make his or her entrance from behind the proscenium arch or through the curtains, up center. I ask the children to move as the mask suggests, and to do one thing that tells us a little more about the character. An angry mask might rip something apart and stamp on it; a silly mask might turn around and look through her legs; a bored mask might kick an imaginary stone across the stage.

As with all rules, even the "no back to the audience" can be broken. I try to establish the rule first, then ask the children to find ways to break it. . .effectively. Here is the kind of thing I've seen happen. A boy entered, up center, back to the audience, and walked backwards down center until we were scared he would fall off the edge of the stage. At the very last minute, he turned around suddenly to show us his "Surprise!" mask face.

And a girl, with long beautiful hair hanging down her back, wearing a full-length slinky dress, entered down left. Keeping her beautiful back to the audience, she moved slowly and sensuously to up center, accompanied, I might add, by wolf whistles and cheers from the audience. Suddenly she ducked her head under her arm, and turning slowly, she revealed her hideous mask! Very clever, very sophisticated, and very funny — especially for a fourteen year old.

As I work with children, I find that one factor above all fascinates and thrills — the Terrible Unknown. Monsters, witches, vampires, werewolves, hulks, robots, Yetis — these are the characters they want to act. Adults often complain that television and movies court our children with tales of evil and horror. While this may be true, I think children have always been interested in the fearful world of dreams and nightmares. We are all vulnerable, and most vulnerable of all when we confront the Unknown.

As a child, I remember my sensuous pleasure in an Arthur Rackham picture of a gruesome giant holding up the blood-dripping head of some poor victim. Our gang of neighborhood children would gather for a special ritual. Slowly we turned over all the pages of that Fairy Tale book until we came to the page before THE page. To our shrieks of anticipated fear and joy the Chief Page Turner would slowly reveal the horrific head and we would all scream and dance around — a marvelous "high!"

Fear — Delicious Fear

Fear must surely be the one emotion most likely to succeed — dramatically. Since the beginning of time, from the baby playing peek-a-boo onward, the human race has carried on a tempestuous love-hate affair with fear. The stone-age man, dancing with the wolf's head, gained power over the animal he had killed, and hid from the unknown spirits he feared. Today's child, at the height of a good theatrical performance, sits literally on the edge of his seat. "Don't let the wolf get her! I can't look!" he screams, hands over his face, fingers parted to see every delicious, scary moment. The stone age child and today's child are not so very far apart on the matter of wolves!

One way of dealing with our fears is to make fun of them, as we will see in Chapter XII, but we can also exorcise them — live through them vicariously — wearing a mask.

The mask has three important powers:

.   The mask wearer feels that he has magical powers over his fears. Masks *are* magical.

.   The mask releases the child's personality by concealing it beneath something very different. The ghastly Frankenstein mask, set on the face of the meekest, shyest child, gives him a chance to be as powerful and awful as he sometimes feels deep inside himself.

.   The mask puts us in touch with feelings we did not even know were there. To express the fear we feel in the pit of our stomachs, to bring it out into the world, brings with it a release, an awareness of creative power, that *needs* to be experienced. Twenty monster-masked children, cavorting around the gym with hands like claws, feet pounding the floor, can be an awesome sight. When the drum has stopped beating and they take off their masks, everyone sits very still. We all know we have been in the world of the unknown.

Monster Masks At Halloween

Of all the festivals we celebrate, Halloween is the oldest. The Druids, priests of ancient Gaul and Britain, celebrated the end of summer with feasting and ritual to scare away evil spirits, ghosts, and witches. Other religions of the world held similar festivals. The Hopi Indians used fearful, masked creatures to punish naughty children, and many primitive people have used masks to scare away disease demons, or the ghosts of the dead. Halloween is obviously a good time of year to start working on monster masks.

I hate the nasty, dull plastic masks that can be bought in dime stores around the beginning of October. Monster masks are such fun to make, and each monster can be unique and terrible in its own way. It seems a pity to me that the most children are likely to do with a scary mask at Halloween is to yell "Trick or Treat!" through it. For many children, Halloween is the most exciting of festivals, because at last there is a ritual for which *they* dress up and participate. Unfortunately, a great deal of the fun has gone out of Halloween because the "Trick" part often degenerates into vandalism, and the "Treat" part can end up as one big stomach ache. Home-made masks — and mask plays — can put some of the fun back into the "witching" festival.

Make-up is a Mask

The papier-mache masks described earlier can be easily adapted for witches and wizards. You will need a long nose, funny teeth, perhaps a wart or two, and a wig of long, dusty hair. But for the best Halloween monsters of all, paint on your own mask with theatrical make-up.

Look for "Theatre-make-up Supplies" in the yellow pages of your telephone book. For witches you will need *green, black,* and *purple* — perhaps also *white.* For a professional long nose, you will need *nose putty* and *spirit gum.* Most people can rustle

Wrinkles

Shadows in
green, blue,
purple, mauve

White highlight
to make cheekbones stand out

Nose putty

Blackened teeth

up an old wig and make it "witchy." For a wizard a beard (perhaps cut from an old wig, or bought at a Tricks and Magic store) is also fun.

A group of children can all learn how to apply witch's make-up, just as they all learn how to put on clown's make-up. The make-up for a witch is basically that of an old person, and for this we borrow the techniques of the Old Masters. Bring in some of the portraits of old people by Rembrandt, such as his self portraits as an old man, or Holbein, or any painting in which the children can look for the shadows and highlights that come with old age.

Put on the nose putty first, and also any warts, using the spirit gum. Roll out the nose first, then model it over the bridge of the child's nose, and finally attach it with a little spirit gum to make sure it stays where you want it. The picture above will give you ideas for how to apply the make-up once you have your nose. Do not forget the neck — and the hands. Long nails are great. . .but a nuisance to apply.

If you have more than one witch, you may want to use basically the same style, but in different shades. I once made up the three witches for a production of *Macbeth*, one in blue, one green, and one purple. It was very effective.

If you cannot find enough old wigs for the whole class, another project is to make witch's hair out of yarn, string, or even paper. For a magic wand, or the handle of a broomstick, take a sheet of newspaper. Starting in the corner, roll it up tightly until you have a wand. Secure the end with scotch tape, and decorate as you wish.

A Scenario To Put Witches into Action

With your room full of witches and wizards, the excitement level will be high. You must channel this energy into good movement, or you may be climbing the walls to make a hasty getaway! Put on some spooky music and start the story.

> Fly through the air on broomsticks on a cold October night. . . way past the moon. . .looking down chimneys. Land on the church steeple and visit the bats in the belfry, and fly to the land of the Enchanted Forest where the ghosts dance nightly on the stroke of midnight.
>
> Back home, you look everywhere for your black cat. At last you find her and pet her and feed her on little (terrible!) tidbits. Now you must set to work, so look through the shelves until you find the book with the right magic spells. Fetch your black cauldron, and gather all the necessary ingredients.

Read the children the list of ingredients the witches used in *Macbeth* (Act IV, Scene 1).

> Round about the cauldron go;
> In the poison'd entrails throw
> Toad that under cold stone
> Days and nights has thirty-one
> Swelt'red venom sleeping got
> Boil thou first i' th' charmed pot.
>
> Double, double toil and trouble;
> Fire burn, and cauldron bubble.
>
> Fillet of a fenny snake,
> In the cauldron boil and bake;
> Eye of newt, and toe of frog,
> Wool of bat, and tongue of dog,
> Adder's fork, and blind-worm's sting,
> Lizard's leg, and howlet's wing —
> For a charm of powr'ful trouble
> Like a hell-broth boil and bubble. . .

At last, when the "charm is firm and good," the children make their spells with a swoosh of their magic sticks.

Many famous witches can be mimed to music or narration. Here are a few that have worked for me:

. The Witch in Hansel and Gretel
. The Russian Witch Baba-Yaga (use the "Baba Yaga" section of Mussorgsky's *Pictures at an Exhibition.*
. The Wicked Witch of the West, from the *Wizard of Oz.*
. The Stepmother in *Snow White and the Seven Dwarfs.*
. The Sea-Witch from "The Little Mermaid."

There are some excellent Witch poems in *"Witch Poems"* (edited by Daisy Wallace, Holiday House, 1976.) Let the children read or recite the poems, either alone or in unison, and then turn up the record player to such music as

. Dukas, *The Sorcerer's Apprentice*
. Mussorgsky, *Night on Bald Mountain*
. Berlioz, The Dream of a Witches' Sabbath, from *Symphonie Fantastique.*
. Saint-Saens, *Danse Macabre*
. Stravinsky, *Fire Bird*

A Good Scenario for One Witch and Lots of Flowers

If you have decided that the thought of making-up and controlling a whole class of witches is beyond you, here is a story about *one* witch and a whole lot of other characters, some with masks, some without.

"The Witch who Loved Flowers (and *Hated* Children!)"

A small group of chilren are playing outdoors — tag; duck-duck-goose; Who Stole the Cookie from the Cookie Jar?; hopscotch, leap-frog; jump rope. There is one child in the group who *whistles* all through the games. They start quarreling and one girl goes off on her high horse — she's mad! The other children continue the games until, with an almighty scream, a witch appears. With her magic wand she freezes all the children. She looks like a ordinary witch except for all the drooping, dead flowers she wears — in her hat, her hair, her cloak, even round her magic wand. With a wicked laugh, she carries off the chilren one by one to her greenhouse, where she turns them all into flowers (by adding a paper-plate flower mask) and sticks them into flower pots. Two children — one of them the whistling child — are left. She converts them into flower-pots (body masks; you can use old plastic garbage cans). The witch waters the flowers, sprays them with insect-killer, pinches some of their leaves, smells them, and then sings them a little song. This is enough to make them all wilt at once! She flies off on her broom-stick.

Enter the girl who left "on her high horse," looking for her friends. She looks everywhere, and is just about to leave when the flower pot begins to whistle. She comes back, suspicious, and examines all the flowers. At this moment, the witch's cat (with cat mask) enters, and the girl realizes what has happened. She thinks for a moment, makes friends with the witch's cat, and, as the witch comes back, the girl and the cat snatch her magic wand. The girl waves the wand over the witch; she freezes. The flowers unfreeze and take off their masks. They turn the witch into a giant-size packet of seeds (Witchweed!) (For this you will need a *huge* paper bag body mask, which is slipped over the head of the witch.) The children play "Duck-duck-goose" all around the Witchweed.

I realize that witches and wizards do not make all of Halloween. Cats and bats are considered with Animal Masks, and many of the monsters in the rest of the chapter will do very nicely for Halloween. But I still consider the "star", the leading role, to be the witch. Supporting this glorious character we may add all kinds of ghosts. These are considered in the chapter on Body Masks, because a good ghost costume should really cover the whole body.

Nowadays, another kind of monstrous creature is flying through space, not on a broomstick, but on a flying saucer, or a space ship. So let us now consider —

Out-of-Space Monster Masks — Paper Bags

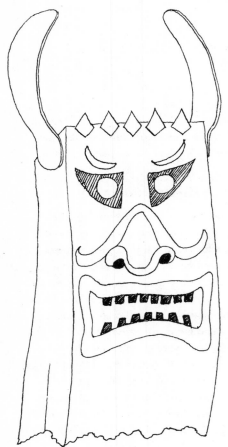

Paper bags — just plain brown shopping bags — make very effective monster masks. Human beings are curvaceous creatures, so the hard, straight lines of a bag immediately suggest something monstrous, un-human. The best size is the super-market shopping bag you get when you are carrying out just a carton of milk and a loaf of bread. The bag should fit snugly over the face. I have·found that super-markets will sell you a quantity of these bags for as little as 25 cents. When you think of what you can create for 25 cents, it's a remarkable bargain!

Let each child try on a bag, and then have a friend mark the correct position for the eyes (and nose and mouth, if you wish). Evil eyes should slant upwards. If you make slits at the 4 corners of the bottom of the bag, the mask will sit comfortably on the shoulders. The children can then paint their masks in bright colors, and add pipe-cleaners, yarn, bottle tops, aluminum pie plates, or anything else they can think of for antennae, dials, hair, etc.

Boxes

The child who discards the expensive gift-toy in favor of putting the box on her head is trying to tell us something! (Also, please note, half the time she is clowning around with the box on her head; the other half, she is playing monster or robot.)

Boxes have the advantage of being interesting to look at from all four sides, and even the top. Also, they provide a good strong base for anything that might be pushed through, stuck on, or otherwise embellish the mask. Do not discard the the styro-foam packaging that comes with various household appliances, like toasters or radios. Some of the packaging, by shape, may already have a sub-human appearane, so you can use it as it comes from the box, or cut and glue different parts onto a base (like a box) The styrofoam can also be painted in different colors.

Cylinders of Paper

Just a sheet of paper, large enough to fit around the head and be securely fastened with staples, makes a different monster mask shape. . .perhaps from another planet? Mark the eyes in the same way as you would a box or the paper bag, and embellish. This mask fits over the top of the head, and is quick and easy to put on.

Before you start your out-of-space masks, it is a good idea to sit down and discuss the Universe. What makes us fascinated and afraid? What do you really think is out there? Do you believe in flying saucers? Robots? Space monsters? Will they ever take over the earth? How do they really move? What sounds might they make?

A good entrance is essential for any kind of monster mask. It should have a shock element, which makes the audience scream "Oooh! ooh!" So, after some general movement, perhaps accompanied by electronic music, with all the children wearing the masks, give each child an opportunity to suddenly appear from behind a flying saucer (blackboard) or the edge of the moon (gym risers) wearing the mask and being as scary as possible. This way everyone has a chance to be an individual monster.

Chorus Work With Masks

If you are working with a class, and all the children have made, for example, paper bag masks of various monsters, but all basically the same kind of creature, then you must think in terms of chorus work. In this you follow directly in the steps of Thespis, and therefore you and your masked monsters are carrying on a very ancient dramatic tradition!

Thespis had his masked chorus sing and dance, often about the heavens and earth and the meaning of life. Your masked monsters will be doing much the same thing. Nowadays children know more than we do about most science fiction, especially space stories, so consult them for possible themes and stories. Here are some ideas I have worked with:

"**Martians Visit Earth**" (for younger children)

To robot sounds (made by the children), a group of Martians are all exploring the craters of the moon, when suddenly a flying saucer comes into view. (Use a bleep-bleep sound, or a flying, high-pitched whistle.) The robots, some reluctantly, leave the moon, and climb into the flying saucer. They whiz through space, past shooting stars and planets, until at last they land on earth. (Earth is wherever the teacher happens to be.) The teacher, as chief Martian, tells them through computer language to explore earth and bring back something interesting when they report to the flying saucer. At the signal from the flying saucer, they all whiz back through space to Mars. It's hot there, and the Martians feel happy to be home. They take turns to report back (in Martian language and robot movement) on what they have seen.

If you have any spare unmasked children (we used three late-comers) they might be captured and brought back to Mars as part of the exhibition.

One night I was sleeping.
Suddenly I heard something. I
looked out the window. There was
a red flashing light that almost
blinded me. I was scared because
I knew it was a spaceship! I
fainted on to the ground. The
noise stared getting louder so
I woke up. I ran out my front
door. I looked around and saw
a door open from the spaceship.
Something walked out. It stared
at me so I stared back. It had
a square nose, no lips, one eye, and
it was bald! Suddenly more and
more creatures came out. They
were friendly so I asked them
if I could go in theire spaceship.
They let me in. Suddenly I had
a sqaure nose, my lips weren't there,
and one of my eyes disappeared,
and I was bald! I knew I turned
into a creature.

By Sioban Dixon

If you are working in a school with, for example, two kindergarten classes, one set of masked monsters might travel through the corridors to visit the "earth creatures" next door, examining this strange phenomenom — a class room — and its even stranger occupants!

Chorus Masks for Older Children

The word Robot came first from the Czechoslovakian play written in 1921 by Karel Capek, "R.U.R.", or "Rossum's Universal Robots", an industrial organization that mass-produces mechanical figures capable of acting as slaves of men. Gradually the robots rise in rebellion against man — and the world, it seems, is doomed to a wholly mechanical existence. At the end of the play, there appears the first glimmerings of love between the two mechanical hearts of the robots — so out of the mechanistic, life is reborn — and with it the first "good" robots. The play is seldom produced nowadays, but the story line of the play makes for excellent mime with older children — and they are usually interested in the origins of robots. There are many other famous science fiction stories — including whole choruses of monsters or robots. Discuss the main plot — extract the action — and use such famous stories as "The War of the Worlds" by H.G. Wells or "The First Men in the Moon" also by H.G. Wells. "From Earth to Moon" by Jules Verne, or "The Princess of Mars" by John Caster. I need hardly say that both "Star Wars" and "Close Encounters of a Third Kind" make good mime plays.

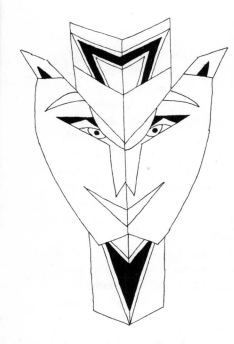

If a small group of children *only* will be wearing the monster masks, then opposite is a story one of my seven-year-old students wrote for our class to perform.

Do not neglect the use of music with any kind of out-of-space story. Although I have found any kind of electronic or synthesized music very effective, I have also used the most unlikely music and found it strangly exciting. I was prompted to do this by my first science fiction movie "2001" where Kubrick uses Richard Strauss' "Thus Spake Zarathustra" and Johann Strauss's waltz tunes with such magnificent results. Often the mood is set by the right use of music as we discussed at the end of chapter 1, and that music may be "right" in an original and different way. Here is a list of music I have used with out of space masks: 1) Prokofiev's ballet "Romeo & Juliet"; 2) Sound track to "Gone with the Wind"; 3) Sibelius "Finlandia"; 4) "Ride of the Valkyries" — Wagner; 5) by popular demand — sound track to "Star Wars".

Monsters From This Earth

Let us now suppose that we are dealing with a very different kind of monster — not a witch, not an airy creature from out of space — but one of the inhabitants of this earth, maybe even a creature like a troll, or a devil, who lives *under* the earth. Some of these earthbound creatures may evolve from animals: real, prehistoric or imaginary, and some of these may be hybrid creatures like griffins, dragons, minataurs, unicorns or gargoyles — the kind of crazy creatures that adorn the roofs and doors of medieval cathedrals. Still other monsters belong to the water, and these seabeasts have developed from the myth of King Neptune, the tales of mermaids and sharks, the legends of Loch Ness, and the gloomy creatures of the primeval swamps. Every country and civilization has developed spirits, evil and not so evil, who inhabit this earth of ours, intruding on the "daily round and common task" with their tricks. Just recently, we have developed a whole host of "friendly" monsters with a passion for cookies or trash, but still they keep their criminal characteristics and still they are ugly, not entirely human.

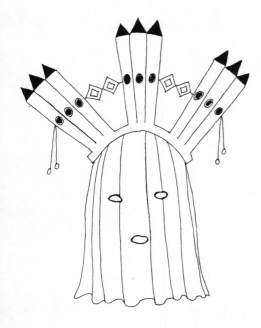

First, then, how to make your mask. I hesitate to specify because we are confronted with so many possibilities. I have used paper bags, styrofoam, papier mache, egg boxes, corrugated cardboard, real boxes, aluminum foil, all to good effect. However, I feel the most successful masks were usually made of cloth. We cut out a hood from some basic fabric in plain color, made eyes, mouth, in the usual fashion, and then added ears, horns, teeth, tusks, antennae, and so forth. Many of the masks featured strangely shaped heads stuffed with foam rubber, so you must consider the size and shape of the monster before cutting your cloth. I asked the children to bring in a collection of fake animal parts, or materials that might be made into tails, claws, hair, fur, teeth, and tusks; Old pieces of fake fur, old wigs, yarn that can be made into tails, old stockings stuffed with paper for ears and tails, yarn, buttons, or curtain rings, string, pipe cleaners, feathers, seashells, even seaweed. Remember too that a tail, some wings, or some gloves with long nails, or claws attached may add a special attraction to your earth monster. As with the monsters from out of space, let us first consider a whole class all working on the same kind of mask — a chorus.

What do the best/worst of the earth monsters do? Pound through the primeval forests, tear apart cities, eat whole trees for lunch, sleep in the craters of volcanos, or up in the Himalayas. Some run about on all fours, others creep along the earth, some fly with wings, snorting and breathing fire through their nostrils. A day in the life of an earth monster could include many adventures. If you consider famous monsters of our time: King Kong, Spiderman, Sasquatch, the Loch Ness Monster, Godzilla, The Wolf Man, The Invisible Man, Dracula, Frankenstein — all of these suggest masks and movement. Children know a great deal about earth monsters too, particularly the ones mentioned above. I have a boy in one class whose father had a collection of the old science fiction comic strips of the Fifties with such characters as Buck Rogers, Flash Gordon, the Tigrone, the Treemen, the Hawkmen, and the Rockmen (moving masses of living clay!). We made masks of all these characters and mimed the perilous and extravagant adventures from some of the comic strips. It was a highly successful class. My own particular interest lies in the monsters of ancient civilizations, and here — at last — I know more than the children! I feel more at home with unicorns and griffins than Godzilla and King Kong! However, I do admit the children's knowledge of dinosaurs far surpasses my own. The range of earth creatures of all *un*human kinds is so vast if we look back over history and cast our eyes upon other civilizations, that we are confronted with a richness of characterization that exceeds the two-footed animal by far.

"Where the Wild Things Are", adapted from the story by Maurice Sendak

This excellent and beloved story with wonderful drawings, just begs for dramatization with masks, and is especially appealing to younger children. In the story, a little boy, Max, tries on a wolf suit (this is your only non-chorus mask — refer to the chapter on animal masks for wolves). Like his ancestors many milleniums back in time, the moment Max tries on that wolf suit, he becomes very wild and wicked, so much so that his mother (I played this dreary role!) banishes him to his room. The room at once turns into a terrible forest of trees (use the children for trees). Next, a great ocean appears (again, use the children for the ocean), and Max takes a little boat and paddles across the ocean to where the Wild Things are. (These, of course, are your glorious masked monsters. They have rows of teeth and round, yellow eyes.) Max becomes king of the Wild Things and has many adventures before returning home to his room to find his supper waiting for him, and it is still hot! We used paper cylinder masks, as being easy to put on, especially as I only had twelve children, so they were also the ocean and the forest.

90 Monster Masks

The Iron King's Treasure (a mime for chorus)

Trolls are Scandinavian monsters who live inside the mountains of the fiords of Norway. They are heartless, sometimes vicious, little creatures with long noses, humps on their backs and tails. In Ibsen's play *Peer Gynt*, there are even two-headed trolls (make a double-headed mask, joined at the shoulders, and stuff the artificial head). The music for this mime is (yes, you guessed!) The Hall of the Mountain King from the *Peer Gynt Suite No. 1*, by Grieg.

The Troll King was very rich. He loved gold and crystal, and at night sent his trolls aboveground to steal from humans. The trolls crept along the banks of the fiords until they came to a rich man's house. They clambered up the staircases, and were just stuffing gold and crystal into their huge sacks when "Lightning" (we used a masked figure in white) came flashing through the house, and the Thunder (again, a masked figure, with drums), rolled. Now there is only one person who can scare a troll, and that is the great God of Thunder, Thor. When the trolls heard him, they dropped all the gold and crystal. All the noise awoke the rich man's little daugher, and she went to investigate. The trolls, in fright, kidnapped the child and took her back to the Mountain King, hotly pursued by "Lightning" and "Thunder."

In the *Peer Gynt Suite* "Anitra's Dance" follows, and this will do very well for your ending. I did this mime many years ago, and although I have listened to the music over again, I cannot remember what happened to the little girl the trolls kidnapped. I suggest you listen to the music with your set of trolls and find your own ending!

Popcorn Devil (a mime for a small group of masked "devils", suitable for younger children)

The Indians believe that inside each kernel of popcorn, there crouches a little devil. When the fire grows hot, so does the popcorn devil, until at last he springs out of the fire.

Divide your group into three —

- Popcorn devils (wearing paper devil masks);

- The fire (children wearing red fire masks, and perhaps carrying sticks with red ribbons or red crepe paper streamers attached);

- Indian children (perhaps with make-up, or at least head-bands and feathers.)

The Fire Masks are crouched together very low in the center, masks hidden. The Indian children are dancing round the fire, until they stop, and set light to the fire. Very slowly the fire begins to smoulder and crackle, and the Fire Masks reveal themselves. Flames dart out, and force the Indian children back. When the fire is hot enough, the Indian children bring in the popcorn (masks hidden). The fire fans the popcorn devils, and they grow bigger and bigger, until one by one they pop all over the place. Each devil is caught by a child and "eaten."

A wonderful accompaniment to this requires careful timing, but is well worth it. Just before you begin your mime, make real popcorn in a corn popper. If the popping and sizzling sounds occur at the same time as your devils are springing out of the fire, you have realistic sound effects — and something delicious to eat when you take off your masks!

Poltergeists (for any age group). Poltergeists are noisy ghosts, so this is not a quiet story for a day when you need something tranquil.

A busy day on an old-fashioned German farm. The milkmaid is milking the cows; the farmer's wife is feeding the chickens, the men are grooming the horses in the stable, and the farmer's children are feeding the pigs. The baby is asleep in its rocking cradle. suddenly, in creep the poltergeists (masked creatures — how about paper plate masks?). All hell breaks loose! The milkmaid is tipped off her stool, and the cow moos in annoyance. The milk pail is spilt and clatters all over the place. The poltergeists throw stones at the horses and make them rear; they steal the grain from the farmer's wife and play games with her big wooden bowl. They put the baby in the pig pen (it yells of course) and the pig in the rocking cradle, and everyone is chasing round and round. Somebody has to figure out how to get rid of the poltergeists.

St. George And The Dragon (a mime for three students)

I based this mime on the famous painting of this name by Paolo Uccello in the National Gallery in London. It has the most terrifying dragon imaginable.

St. George (in armor, with an aluminum foil mask) comes in on his charger seeking the lair of the wicked dragon. This cruel monster lived in a lake (something like the Loch Ness monster) and menaced the town nearby. In spite of offerings of sheep and cows, the dragon had an insatiable appetite and went on eating humans. Fortunately, St. George comes by on his charger just as the dragon is about to consume a beautiful princess. Wounded, the dragon becomes submissive, and St. George bids the Princess fasten her girdle around its neck, so that they can lead it off into the town.

"Punchinella, Punchinella, what can you do?" In an old children's game, played in South Carolina for as long as my friend, Delores, can remember, whoever jumps into the circle as Punchinella has to perform tricks which everyone copies. And who is Punchinella? One of the oldest, the original clowns.

We do not know exactly how the groups of travelling players known as the Commedia dell' Arte developed in Italy in the 16th century, but we do know that the stock characters they played — Punchinella, Harlequin, Columbina, Pantelone, Pagliacci — have their origins back in the Roman times, and that the Romans derived them from the Greeks! So the children in South Carolina are playing with a tradition that is thousands of years old.

I have taught children as young as seven years old all about the Commedia dell' Arte. They are always fascinated. All children love circuses, and most children love the clowns best of all, so the history of clowns is most interesting to them. I consider it a valuable piece of knowledge anyway. It is also the best introduction I know to clown make-up and masks. Several of the characters of the Commedia were called "The Masks," in fact. I find work on the Commedia an excellent way to introduce funny masks. It ties together character and comedy work in a beautiful way.

All the Commedia plays were improvised from a scenario — tacked up in the wings of the portable stage, and as the players travelled from north to south in Italy, and then throughout Europe, they relied on mime as their main means of communication. The dialects of Naples were hardly understood by the Florentines in the north, so the players improvised a language of gesture that could be readily understood by all. Remember, these actors were Italians, so to speak with their hands came easily and readily.

I should also add that at a time when all Shakespeare's heroines were played by male actors, in the Commedia dell' Arte troupes, actresses not only played the female roles, but in some cases were even the leaders of the troupe. Isabella Andrieni was one of the first great actor-managers.

Just as in today's television serials, the actor always played the same character. He was immediately recognizable by his costume, mask or make-up, and his movement. As I describe the different characters and the kind of story that they improvised, you will also see why the Commedia dell' Arte has had far-reaching influences on circuses, ballet, opera, mime, art and music. We know that Shakespeare saw them, because he borrowed several of their stories for his plays (*The Tempest,* for example) Moliere wrote several of his most famous comedies after the Italian players arrived in Paris. In Denmark, today, there are still Commedia dell' Arte players whose origins go back to the 17th century.

The characters and their masks

Let us begin with **Punchinella**. In England, this character has passed into the puppet world, as half of the "Punch and Judy" team. There is still a magazine — *Punch* — named after him.

Punchinella comes from Naples, so he has southern temperament. His hunchbacked appearance, long-nosed mask, and wooden dagger make him quite a sinister character, but, like the famous "Hunchback of Notre Dame," his outward appearance often conceals a good heart. He would share his last crumb of bread with anyone.

When children try out this character, I get them to make a black mask, and put some kind of hump on their back. We discover that the world is quite different from the point of view of a hunchback. For one thing, you always have to look *up* to people from your stooped position. Punchinella can sometimes be mean (in Punch and Judy shows he is always beating the baby with his cudgel!) and he has a coarse, bird-like laugh as he sets about his intrigues. He is often a servant, pushed around by his "masters."

Harlequin originally wore a costume that was a patchwork of different animal skins, but eventually it developed into the multi-colored suit and the black half-mask.

Harlequin is a great acrobat, great lover, and a great trickster. He loves to swing his magic baton as he sneaks through imaginary windows, insolent and lively. I see many Harlequins in schools all over the place!

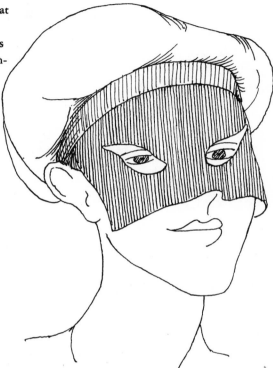

Pagliacci (in France, **Pierrot**; and in Russian, **Petrouchka**) is perhaps the most famous Commedia dell' Arte character. He is the original sad clown.

Leoncavallo uses him in the famous opera, *Pagliacci*, featuring a 19th century Commedia troupe. Pierrot has captured the imagination of painters like Renoir, Degas, Cezanne, and Picasso. In our own century Marcel Marceau has borrowed his white face and whimsical ways for his famous character "Bip." Charlie Chaplin, Buster Keaton and Woody Allen have all played Pierrot for his pathos. He is the original underdog and, as such, the subject of universal empathy. The French-style Pierrot is also the great romantic.

My own belief is that this pale-faced adolescent joined one of the well-established Commedia troupes as a servant, and eventually was pushed on stage, still clutching his broom and bucket. Everyone laughed, but Pierrot, melancholy youth, can only sigh — and trip over his bucket of water. Poor Pierrot is full of love and, of course, such characters as Columbine will flirt with him, but he is never successful like Harlequin.

El Capitano (The Captain) is the braggart soldier. (Remember him as Miles Gloriosos in *A Funny Thing Happened on the Way to The Forum?*) At heart he is really a coward, but he loves to think himself the world's greatest soldier. . .lover. . .and leader. He will boast of mighty battles, but the sight of a sword in the hands of Harlequin will send him rushing off-stage clutching his pants! W.C. Fields has carried on his tradition in this century.

Isabella is the beautiful Heroine — beloved of the Hero. A nice lady . . . we see her in hundreds of plays and operas (Olivia in Shakespeare's *Twelfth Night*; Julie Andrews is still playing her role today). Kind and rich and good and, for my money, not much fun, but there are always scores of little girls who want to play Cinderella. Personally I prefer the ugly step-sisters!

Columbine — the "soubrette" role. Quick and full of sass, a dancer, a flirt, Columbine was usually the maid to the lady of the house. She enjoyed life and had many lovers; and she was often beloved of Harlequin.

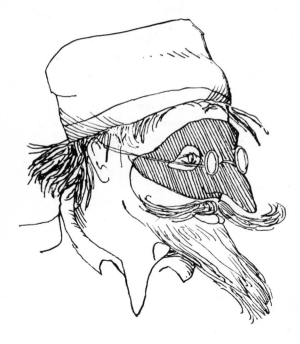

Pantaloon. Shakespeare described him in *As You Like It:*

> The sixth age, shifts into the lean and
> slippered Pantaloon,
> With spectacles on nose, and pouch
> on side.
> His youthful hose, well saved, a world
> too wide
> For his shrunk shank.

Pantalone (the origin for the word "pants") is the archetypal dithering old idiot, usually somebody's ancient father. A ridiculous, miserly, old man, he usually spends half his time complaining about his aches and pains! He walks with his toes turned in — and wears a half-mask.

These are some of the main characters. You might also like to include Scapino (the original villain — all dressed in black, and playing his guitar in sinister fashion); The Doctor (the quack, who talks too much, using long gibberish words, and carries a bag full of terrible potions) and The Hero (a stiff, upright, young gentleman, useful only as a foil to other characters, and the lover of Isabella).

When I describe the Commedia characters to the children, I like to spend some time in movement and comic routines for each character before we decide who plays which role. Refer back to the section on character "walks" (pp. 26-29) to help find the swaggering Captain, the light and tricky Harlequin, the flirtatious Columbine, and the shuffling old Pantalone. Then we make masks, or use make-up, and begin work on. . .

Lazzi

The Commedia dell' Arte players could each perform a series of "lazzis" — funny routines that could be thrown into a scenario whenever the action was lagging. Many of them were handed down from one generation of characters to the next, in the way that several clown routines have become famous today.

Here are some "lazzis" for you different characters to try, once you have found the walk, and made a mask (or make-up).

Columbine

. She tries on make-up belonging to her mistress — lots of powders, perfume, eyelashes, and various jewels. Suddenly, she hears her mistress coming, and pretends to be dusting with a feather duster.

. (with Pantalone). Columbine tries to get as much money out of the old man as she possibly can. Her stockings are full of holes; she is hungry; she needs ribbons, gloves. She gives him kisses and even promises to marry him. He asks, "Do you love me?" and she says (after safely pocketing the money) "I would, but I have one, two, three, four, five children at home and husband!"

Harlequin

. **The Lazzi of the Cherries.** Harlequin enters with a big bag of something delicious to eat. At last he shows the audience. . . it's cherries! He takes them out and eats them with great ceremony — spitting the pits at the audience. He then blows up the paper bag and pops it.

. Harlequin brings in a ladder. He is going to put up a poster on a high wall. Every time he gets one corner well and truly stuck, the other one falls down. He also has some fun with the imaginary ladder. . .wobbling. . .being scared of the height. . .doing acrobatic tricks.

Pantalone

. He is counting all his money, but keeps dropping and losing it, forgetting where he put it. His spectacles fall off his nose, and he shuffles back and forth to an imaginary cupboard where he locks all his money. Then he forgets where he put the key.

. Pantalone is cleaning eyeglasses, with great precision. At last we realize there's no glass in the frames, because he pulls the cloth through the hole with his teeth.

Pierrot

. The love letter he is writing gives him *great* problems. He keeps tearing up one letter, and starting afresh. Suddenly he has a wonderful idea, but it makes him shy so he hides it from the audience. When it's finally finished he reads it and thinks it quite beautiful. Suddenly he sees Columbine appear. He kneels and offers the letter. . .but she tosses it aside and laughs when she reads it.

. One story tells us that Pierrot was born out of the moon. Let someone whistle the French folk song, "Au Clair de la Lune, Mon Ami Pierrot" as background for this lazzi.

Pierrot slowly uncurls and emerges from the moon. He sees stars, planets, and finally the world. He wants it, tries to reach it, but the only way he can do so is to leap into space. He lands on earth, and explores flowers, trees and water. Finally he sees his own reflection in the water and plays games with it. Then he becomes angry because he can't reach "his friend."

Isabella

. She is arranging flowers when suddenly a fly is buzzing around her head. She tries to catch the fly. When eventually she does so, she gives him a lecture: "Don't go near my flowers!" The fly replies, but she cannot hear him so she puts him close to her ear and listens to his talk. He makes her feel so sorry for him that she sends him (gently) off into the audience. (Use imaginary fly.)

. She climbs up, round and up, up and round, a long medieval-style staircase, until she comes to a closet that contains her imaginary jewels. She tries them all on, puts them all in an imaginary box, and goes round and down, and down and round, and round and down until she reaches a door which leads out to the audience. She gives all the jewels to different members of the audience.

Captain

. He is cleaning his sword, admiring himself in an
imaginary mirror, getting all ready for a duel.
Suddenly, as he is practicing a great flourish, he sees
his opponent, and runs away in fear!

. He is putting on a whole row of medals for bravery,
polishing them, admiring himself, when a little
mouse appears. He thinks it's a monster, jumps up on
a chair, quakes with fear, and drops all his medals.

Punchinella

. (For this, make a rag doll the same size as the actor, out of an
old pair of pants and a shirt stuffed with newspaper, and add
a masked head with a hat. Tie the feet of the doll to the feet
of Punchinella, and put on some Italian music, preferably
Neopolitan.)

Punchinella does a loving dance with the doll, pretending she
is real. At the end of the dance he keeps kissing her, trying
to make her come to life, and then, and only then, does he
realize that she is only a doll.

. Two guards come in to take Punchinella to prison. He says,
"First I must tie my shoelaces." He bends down, grabs the legs
of the two guards, trips them up, and escapes.

A Scenario for a Commedia Play

This story line is the kind of outline that might be tacked up in the wings a few
hours before a Commedia performance. After I have taught the Commedia characters
and we have all enjoyed doing the lazzis together, I let the children cast one another.
I am always interested in their choices, because they are usually exactly the same as
mine. I like to give them a few examples of the kind of story they might act out —
and then I tack up three or four scenarios at strategic points in the room and give them
time to act them out.

~HOW HARLEQUIN WON COLUMBINE~

Characters: Columbine   Captain
Harlequin   Punchinello

Columbine is getting ready to go to a party. Just as she is pulling the garter up her leg, Harlequin enters. His eye goes up and down her leg. He tells her he loves her and the two are just about to run away together, when Punchinello enters. He pushes Columbine back inside, throws Harlequin out, and locks the door with a big key. Columbine sticks out her tongue and sits down to sulk. Harlequin, meanwhile, on the other side of the door, does the lazzi of the cherries.

Enter the Captain, with a huge bunch of flowers for Columbine. He tries the door, and cannot open it. So he decides to write her a letter. Harlequin is looking over his shoulders all the time! As the Captain slides the letter under the door, Harlequin surprises him, and he nearly faints.

Harlequin and the Captain fight -- with swords -- until the Captain is on his knees, begging for mercy. He promises to help Harlequin win Columbine. Harlequin lets him go, and the Captain goes off to get a ladder. He keeps falling over his cloak, but eventually, with big, exaggerated steps, they place the ladder under Columbine's window. She runs to the window, delighted to see Harlequin. The Captain holds the ladder while Harlequin climbs.

Enter Punchinello. He is furious, and tries to kill the Captain. The Captain says, "I'll give you all my money." Now Punchinello asks Harlequin for money, but he shows that he has no money. Punchinello demands to see the Captain's money. While they are counting it out -- and quarreling -- Harlequin and Columbine slip away!

Georges Rouault, the famous French painter, writing about his art in 1903, told the following story —

> I saw a gypsy wagon halted at the side of the road, a weary old horse nibbling
> stunted grass, an old clown patching his costume; the contrast, in fact, between
> the brilliance and scintillation of laughter, and the intense sadness of life itself.
> I saw quite clearly that the clown was myself, all of us. . .the gaudy spangled
> dress was what life gives us. We all wear a spangled dress of some sort, but
> if someone catches us with the spangles off, as I caught that old clown — oh,
> the infinite pity of it.

We all need time for more spangles. Not only the clown in every group, but also the ones who wish they could be clowns too. Just recently, there has been a revival of interest in clowns. Everywhere I see clown workshops for children, and library books full of ideas about how to start your own circus, or perform magic tricks, or fool your friends. Shopping centers and fairs have little booths set up where a clown will make up a child for a few dollars.

Modern circus clowns have abandoned the mask for make-up. But just as with the Witch, the clown's make-up is indeed a kind of mask, a very flexible one, and part of the ancient tradition of wearing more than your everyday face for a special holiday occasion.

The clown is a direct descendant of the Medieval jester. Dressed in his parti-colored costume, shaking his stick with bells to attract attention, juggling, tumbling, clowning regardless of how he felt, the jester was employed to make others feel happy. The Fools of the era did not always live at court. Some of them travelled to fairs and marketplaces all over the world. And nowadays the circus is still travelling with its clowns. Wherever they travel. . .from Medieval banquet halls to Madison Square Garden. . .there is too much noise, too much hustle and bustle for lengthy, concentrated, witty dialogue. So what is a clown to do? Mime!

Making Up Clowns

I start with the make-up rather than the movement. You need make-up on to feel like a clown. My friend, Celeste Zagarola, has a very good introduction to clown make-up for younger children. I have watched her do it, and the children are enthralled. She brings to class

> A mirror
> White clown make-up
> A black and a red liner
> A funny nose
> Wig
> Full clown costume, including a pillow to make her look fat, and enormous
>   shoes.

Slowly, before their eyes, she transforms herself from a teacher into a clown. She adeptly draws the children into the experience by discussing how the make-up feels. "What kind of clown would you like?. . .sad or happy? Would you please help with these big shoes. . .I can't see my feet past my stomach."

When the make-up and costume were complete, I asked the children, "Where is Mrs. Zagarola? "She left," they replied. For these children, the metamorphosis was complete. The teacher then made up as many children as wished to be clowns, put on some clown music, and they danced around the room and down the hallways — a happy sight!

Older children will enjoy putting on their own make-up. There are basically three types of clown. Let the children decide on their own "kind of clown." Of course, there are many varieties within these three characters. Children who know something of Commedia dell' Arte will understand this.

Whiteface

He is derived from the characters of Harlequin and Punchinella. The make-up is basically white and smooth, with no great exaggeration of the features. The eyebrows, nose and mouth are painted in combinations of red and black. This is a very good make-up for children to try. "Whiteface" wears a conical hat and gorgeous spangled outfit. He is usually the boss. It is Whiteface who throws all the custard pies. In a dentist routine, he is always the one who pulls the tooth, never the poor patient. When Whiteface makes a funny joke, he is so pleased with himself that he jumps up and down for joy, hugs himself, and turns cartwheels.

Character Clown

This very special clown is usually the star of the circus, and he often does a solo routine. This is the make-up for the *real* clown in your group — the one with individuality and a style all his own. Famous clowns like Emmet Kelly spent years finding their particular character. This famous tramp clown tries to sweep the area with a big broom and has all kinds of antics trying to sweep up the spotlight. Coco the Clown, another famous character clown, developed acts where buckets of water were thrown about, and Coco received most of them on his head. Felix Adler developed special acts with animals, and liked to make believe he could control a cage full of tigers and lions.

Auguste

The word comes from the German meaning clumsy boy. The Auguste make-up is the maddest in the whole circus: a big red mouth, a false red nose, tufts of hair sticking up from either side of his face. Everything he wears is grotesque and out of proportion. . .huge pointed shoes, baggy pants, a tiny hat perched on his head. He is the clown responsible for most of the slapstick, and he is definitely the one in the dentist chair and the butt for all flying pies. An Auguste will do almost anything for a laugh. Like his ancestor, poor Pierrot, he doesn't always find it easy. When he is sad he buries his face in his hands, rolls over, and howls into the ground. He then blows his nose on an enormous handkerchief and pokes it right through the hole! He is the most accident prone clown in the whole circus. Traditionally, in England, Auguste carries a string of sausages, a prop developed in the 16th century.

Clown Pantomimes

From the earliest of days of the Greek comic Mimes, the clown has had to rely on visual effects. Today's clowns have perfected these techniques almost to an art form. Many mime schools teach a variety of pantomime tricks, like pulling on imaginary ropes, creating walls and doors and then being imprisoned by them; blowing up balloons and then being carried into the air by them; mime "walks" that create many different illusions. In your work with clowns you might like to work on some of these, but they are almost like dance steps, so you will have to learn how to do them yourself first, in order to demonstrate; or invite a professional Mime on a special visit.

I have certain reservations about teaching this kind of mime myself. It has now become a cliche and, as such, is not truly creative. In the past few years I have seen at least a dozen mime shows featuring the rope pulling episode. It was marvelous the first time Marcel Marceau created that particular trick, but since then half the Mimes in America have copied him.

Here are some ideas I do like to do with a room full of children in clown make-up. First of all I let different style clowns take turns playing "follow the leader." Whatever tricks the leaders do, so do the rest of the clowns. We finish with a grand parade to music like "Bring on the Clowns." I then have a "clown conference" to think of all the funniest tricks in the world. Some of these, of course, will be based on what we remember from visits to the circus, and some will grow from the character of clowns. Some of the ideas we've used in our circuses include

. Clowns playing games all wrong:

> "Ring around the rosy
> Pocket full of posy
> Aitchoo! Aitchoo! (Pause for nonsense with sneezing clown)
> We all fall UP!

. Clowns weightlifting with balloons tied to a stick.
. Clowns juggling — badly!
. One clown with a hat sits on a chair, and the others try to trick him into giving them the hat, but he resists.
. The dentist act

. A clown boxing match with mock muscles and floppy gloves
. One clown winds up another with a huge key as though he is a mechanical toy, but the Toy goes beserk
. Two clowns going around a haunted house
. An old-fashioned photographer comes to take a picture of the other clowns with one of those cameras where you put your head under a cloth
. Barber shop routine. Giant comb, scissors, and shampoo needed.
. A sword fight. Right in the middle of the fight, the clowns do something silly like a very sedate minuet.

Clowns In Other Settings

Outside of the circus there are a host of other Funny Men and Women. Some children seem to be natural clowns. Do you have a funny guy in your group, the one child who makes everyone laugh with his antics? Like many clowns, they may be just wearing a mask and, in truth, be shy, or sad, or troubled underneath. "It's the hap-hap-happy people fall hardest when they break," said Carl Sandburg, so go gently with the clowns in your group. They rely on their masks more than anyone else.

When I plan clown sessions for my classes, I try to remind myself that the things that make children laugh are the very things that tickle adults, namely

Fantasy. Whole comedy routines can come out of such situations as

. 17 clowns all coming out of one Volkswagen
. The Mad Hatter's Tea Party in *Alice in Wonderland*
. All the elephant jokes you ever heard
. The Wicked Witch of the West disappearing into the ground
. Charlie Chaplin eating his boots and spitting out the nails.

Frustration. Another series of comic adventures begin with

. All the corn flakes spilling on the kitchen floor when you are late for school
. Laurel and Hardy, however hard they try to get their house built, encountering one problem on top of another
. Any Little Guy encountering any big Guy in a cartoon
. Lucille Ball trying to conduct a junior choir while one kid keeps rolling toward her on roller skates
. Most of the Ernie/Bert routines on Sesame Street.

Fear. I once asked children to draw me pictures of what they feared most. Here is a list of some of the responses. Most of these fears have the potential for making us laugh, for when I held up the children's pictures and then asked them to mime them, most of the time they turned into funny acts.

. Lying in bed at night in the dark and you think someone is there.
. Falling (Falls have always been funny).
. Everyone laughing at you because your mother made you wear this gross outfit.
. Wolves jumping out from behind the closet.
. Being lost in a shopping center, and you can't find your mother.
. When your parents fight, they might get divorced.
. Always forgetting your library books, homework or lunch money.
. The doctor giving you a shot.

Phobias. If you have an older group, and would like to explore further in this realm, you can build a lesson around phobias. I start with a discussion on what the word means, and then divide the class into groups, giving each one a phobia. I tell them, "Make up a story about one or two people in the group who have this particular phobia. The story should build to a funny ending."

. Claustrophobia, fear of enclosed spaces
. Microphobia, fear of germs
. Acrophobia, fear of heights
. Zoophobia, fear of animals.

I have done this exercise with and without masks. We used simple yellow (color of fear) paper masks worn only by the phobia person. I felt the masked group was more effective. The mask added a stronger definition and helped to spotlight the central character, giving greater emphasis to the comedy.

Ideas For Comic Props

To add one or two funny props is part of the stock-in-trade of the comedian. This may be a full scale funny mask, or something as simple as a moustache such as Charlie Chaplin used, or a wig (Harpo Marx), or eyeglasses (Woody Allen). Two thousand years ago, in the times of the Roman Mimes, the funniest thing a Comic would wear was a giant sized phallus tied around the waist. Another comic prop handed down from the ancients is the Slapstick, a baton or cane for comic slapping routines (hence the origin of the word "Slapstick!") I make slapsticks with children from a sheet of newspaper rolled diagonally, similar to the way we make the witch's wand. This makes a firm, but safe, slapstick for each child.

Collect together a box full of

Funny masks
Wigs made of a variety of materials
Shoes
Eyeglasses, all sizes and colors
Moustaches and Beards
Funny Noses
Canes, Umbrellas, Gloves and Slapsticks

Let each child select his or her funny prop from which to develop a character. Put the children into small groups of twos or threes. One will usually be the "Boss," the others underdogs. Here are some story lines around which to build comic routines using the funny props:

Favorite Jokes and Riddles. Let each group tell their favorite jokes and riddles, and act them out using the Funny Props. Even "knock-knock" jokes are fun for pantomime.

Nursery Rhymes. One of the funniest scenes I ever saw developed from my box of Funny Props via nursery rhymes. I was discussing with a group of sixth grade students the origins of nursery rhymes, their satirical nature, and the extraordinary characters involved. Each child took a prop from the box and became a nursery rhyme character.

In one, Jack Spratt (with droopy moustache) and Mrs. Spratt (with pillow under her sweater) returned to their home to the tune of the wedding march. Mrs. Spratt cooked a delicious meal, and they sat down to eat. A terrific quarrel developed, and Mrs. Spratt chased Jack around the room with a pan. She was just about to whack him, when Jack came up with an idea:

> Jack Spratt could eat no fat
> His wife could eat no lean

So between the two of them
They eat the platter clean.

A different Jack (with vinegar and brown paper) and Jill (with silly wig) tumbled down the hill while fetching a pail of water. A quack doctor came to visit, complete with stethoscope and glasses. The doctor routine can be very funny. You need someone who is good at occupational mime to pull yards of imaginary intestines out of the stomach, etc.

Characters from Literature. Among the famous "clowns" of literature is Till Eulenspiegel, a 16th century German character whose merry pranks are legendary. Since Till did things like tightrope walking on his neighbor's clothes line, his tricks are very suitable for mime. Use the mime with Richard Strauss's *Till Eulenspeigel*. The Tweedledum and Tweedledee scene from *Alice in Wonderland* calls for marvelous props. Another favorite is Puck, from Shakespeare's *Midsummer Night's Dream*.

Good Culminating Scenes for Clowns and Clowning

. A Circus, entirely in mime, using a narrator. There is a marvelous descriptive poem for this purpose called "Circus," by Jack Prelutsky, with beautiful pictures describing tumblers, a monkey band, the strong man, the sword swallower and fire eater, the seals, the trapeze artist, and all varieties of clowns. The poem ends with the Grand Finale Parade.

. Silent Movies. If you can possibly show the children one of the classic comedy silent films, this mime will work better. Work out a story line based on all the old cliches of the first cowboy films. Choose your moustaches, beards, hats, guns and Indian headresses. Put your Bad Guys on one side of the room, Good Guys on the other. Work out some funny business with fights first. Remember that in pretend fights, (and these should be extra phony) it is the one who is being hit who does most of the action. The plot line should be absolutely clear, so write down your cue cards first. You will also need some fast-paced tinkling piano music in the background.

. *The Love of Three Oranges,* based on the Prokofiev opera. Once upon a time there was a prince who would never laugh. The King, his father, was so worried about him that he arranged a meeting with the Court Magician, who suggested a fantastic party to which all kinds of entertainers would be invited. One by one the different entertainers performed before the prince: juggling acts, silly dances, pantomime, songs and jokes, but the prince would not laugh. Suddenly, an uninvited guest appeared: a Wicked Witch. She was furious that she had not been asked, and tried to elude the palace guards as they chased her away; but she tumbled to the floor and turned a somersault. The prince laughed!

Apart from the funny Entertainers, you will also need a straight-faced prince, a worried King, Court Magician, a Witch, and two guards.

While I was working on *The Love of Three Oranges* I asked the children for suggestions for funny tricks. "Do you have anything special that just you can do?" I asked. A little girl in the group offered her deformed hand. Inside of me I cried at the suggestion, but how I admired her courage — and that of the hunch-back jester, the Fattest Lady on Earth, and the midget clowns.

There is always something slightly ludicrous about people in animal costumes. We are rarely the right size for the animal; too large for a rabbit, too small for an elephant. We have all the wrong appendages. . .two legs, not four; no wings; no tail; ears in the wrong place; no whiskers. And the more extravagant animal costumes can cost a small fortune in fake fur.

I am not saying "Never wear an animal costume." But do think twice before you go to a great deal of trouble and expense. Could you not manage with just a mask, a tail, some whiskers, and paws?

As so many good stories and plays for children do involve animal characters, masks often provide the best answer. Apart from being less expensive than the complete costume, the mask affords the child the freedom to move and feel like the animal, Unhampered by a cumbersome costume, the Mime can concentrate on finding the essence of "donkey," for example. . .not just any donkey, but a particular donkey. All donkeys are not the same, just as all people are not the same. If we work with just movement and a mask −− or make-up, ears and tail −− we are free to find individual characteristics for the animal we are playing. When you are playing the back end of a horse, sweltering in some terrific costume, or a crocodile sliding around face down on a skate board (as happened in my production of *Peter Pan*) all your creativity is confined to coping with the costume.

The early ballets and masques of the 17th century often used animal or bird characters. Since the dancer had to be free to move and see, and display the agility of his body, the most imaginative masks were created —— masks that occupied themselves largely with the head, leaving arms and legs free to express the feel of the animal.

Before you begin making the animal masks, one important question must be considered:

How Far Are They Animals: How Far Are They People?

Or, to be practical —— are they animals with clothes and human characteristics, as Babar is in *Babar the Elephant,* or are they "animal animals" as in the story of Noah's Ark?

If your animals are in the first category (i.e. animal people), then my own feeling is that a helmet mask with ears attached and a little make-up, and perhaps the addition of a tail or wings, serves best. But the mask or make-up for either category of animals is the last thing to be added. I like to do a great deal of work in animal mime before finally adding the mask for the festive culminating activity or using it as the costume in a play. In addition to the ideas in Chapter V, here is an interesting exercise, used quite often in acting classes for character development, that is especially useful in preparing a Brer Rabbit or a Tom Kitten. I have used it with children as young as third graders.

Animal—People or People—Animals

Start first by finding the essential movement of an animal, a donkey, let us say.

> You move on four legs, not two. Think about that. How do you move? No pounding, proud clip-clop as for the horse, but something gentler, daintier, closer to the ground. You are covered all over in fur, and your tail is useful in hot weather for swishing away flies. . .but it is your head, that stubborn head with the oversized ears, the braying mouth full of teeth, the bridle you wear because you are so often the servant of Man. . .*this* is the essential donkey. You are one of a mangy pack of donkeys that tread the beaches every summer giving rides to the children. Are you the young, pretty female that all the little girls love to ride? Or the old grey one who should have retired last year, but your owner knows how patient and docile you are? Or are you the biting, frisky one, bored with the tiresome plodding through the sand?

Now that you are an individual, unique donkey, go through your paces for a day on the beach, until night falls and you sleep in the field behind the owner's trailer.

Now suppose this donkey becomes a person —— a complete person —— but keeping his characteristics as a donkey. What sort of a person would he be?

I like to work in this sequence:

1. All the class becomes donkeys —— any donkey —— anywhere.

2. Everyone becomes a particular donkey. It need not be a beach donkey. He or she could live in the mountains of Peru, or in a children's zoo —— but he should be a special donkey.

3. Now everyone turns their special donkey into a person, going through the routine of a hot summer day, from early morning until late at night.

I now ask the children to choose their own animal/bird/insect/fish. We act out that animal, from the time it awakes and looks for food until night. We then turn all these different creatures into people, and I send them off to look for food, or play, or work. I am always interested in the kind of animal a child chooses. It is fun to discuss the affinity the animal has for each child's own personality. I put it this way: "If Bobby weren't Bobby, but an animal, or a bird, or a fish, which one would he be?" (I am a beagle!)

The question that always arises in this exercise is "How far am I a person, how far am I an animal?" My answer is this: if you are using the animal characteristics in order to find a truly *human* character, then it is only a device for finding that person. If, however, you are a storybook animal like Brer Rabbit or Tom Kitten, then it is about 50/50. Find the animal feeling first, then add the mask, tail, whiskers and clothes (if that is what you wear), and the character should evolve. (In some cases, as in the 19th century animal/people of Beatrix Potter, or the Uncle Remus tales, you are also tied to a certain period and environment. Not only must you act like a kitten, you also have to remember you are a 19th century English kitten in "clean pinafore and tucker"!)

Most directors working on scripted plays with animal characters add these characteristics too late in rehearsal time. A mime session should come right at the beginning of the rehearsal period.

Animals—Animals

All animals know how to play — — to mimic. A dog does not paint a picture, a cat cannot appreciate Mozart, and a bird does not decorate its nest, but watch that dog roll over and "play dead" to amuse his master, or the cat with a ball of yarn, or a bird flirting with its mate. It is this mimicry, this delightful zest for living, that makes animals so appealing, especially to children. When we put on a good animal mask, and yet keep our human bodies, we assume this same kind of mimicry — — of animal language.

Before we come to the culmination of putting on the animal/bird/insect/fish mask — — perhaps as the climax of work in animal mime — — it is important to spend time working on the animal in pure mime. Here are some exercises.

- You (a dog) have lived many years in close companionship with an old man. He has just died and the house is locked up. You try every means of escape. . .to no avail. So you sit and wait, for a long time, until eventually someone arrives and takes your master's body away. They give you food and water, but you will not drink or eat. You just find an old slipper belonging to your master, and guard it. (A true story)

- A mother hen is sitting on her nest. She lays three very important eggs. These will be her new brood of chicks. When they hatch, how proud she is.

- A dolphin in a dolphin show is doing all his best tricks for the audience.

- Two birds — — male and female (the masks should help you decide on the species) are courting one another. It is spring — — naturally!

- A lion with a thorn in its paw cannot get it out. What will happen?

- An old pirate (use a scarf mask) and his parrot set out to look for treasure.

How Animal Masks Can Enhance a Production

One of my first experiences with animal masks was when I directed a low-budget production of Andre Obey's beautiful play, *Noah*. The animals in the play do not speak, although they must communicate a great deal, especially with Noah. These are not half-human creatures; they are truly animal.

In the photographs of the Broadway production, the animals had full-scale costumes, and I am sure they were beautiful on a large stage. For my simpler production, performed in a church (converted into an ark) such costumes would have been out of place. Instead we did a great deal of work on animal mime, dressed everyone in black leotards and tights, and used plain white paper (oak-tag) masks. The effect of this inexpensive device was stunning.

Animal masks may also be made of fabric, styrofoam, feathers, fake fur, or even wire. The horse masks for the Broadway production of *Equus*, made simply of wire, were magnificent.

Many stories, particularly fairy tales, come to a climax in the moment of transformation from animal to human. The beast, or the bear, or the frog, becomes a handsome prince. The White Cat turns into a beautiful Princess. The lizard becomes a Cinderella's coachman. If you are going to enact these stories, a mask is absolutely necessary.

One final reason for using animal masks is hard to define, but I will try. After working fairly consistently on animal mime, you come up against a theme, a poem, or a story which requires something *more* than the human body can provide. Look at this poem by Carl Sandburg:

> There is a wolf in me . . . fangs pointed for tearing gashes
> . . . a red tongue for raw meat . . . and the hot lapping
> of blood — I keep this wolf because the wilderness gave it
> to me and the wilderness will not let it go.

There is a fox in me . . . a silver-gray fox . . . I sniff and
guess . . . I pick things out of the wind and air . . . I nose
in the dark night and take sleepers and eat them and hide
the feathers . . . I circle and loop and doublecross.

There is a hog in me . . . a snout and a belly . . . a machinery
for eating and grunting . . . a machinery for sleeping
satisfied in the sun — I got this too from the wilderness and
the wilderness will not let it go.

There is an eagle in me and a mockingbird . . . and the eagle
flies among the Rocky Mountains of my dreams and fights
among the Sierra crags of what I want . . . and the mockingbird warbles in the early forenoon before the dew is
gone, warbles in the underbrush of my Chattanoogas of
hope, gushes over the blue Ozark foothills of my wishes —
And I got the eagle and the mockingbird from the wilderness.

from Wilderness

To interpret the abstract ideas of this poem through movement, one needs the
extension of a mask. While a child, or a group of children, are reading the poem,
a masked wolf, silver-gray fox, hog, eagle, and mocking bird move back and forth
from the central figure (the speaker from "The Wilderness" and the voice of Carl
Sandburg himself.) Projects of this sort are very suitable for teenagers. How many times
have people complained that the difficult teenager is "an animal?" Let him put on
a mask. . .let him become an animal.

Animal Stories Suitable For Simple Masks

Even such animal stories and poems as small children enjoy will be enhanced by simple
masks. They will make the children feel closer to the animal they are portraying, and
if the work has been preceded by good mime, without masks, you will discover a
performance level that can be quite remarkable to watch. All the following stories
lend themselves to masks:

.   *The Bremen Town Musicians*
.   *The Little Rabbit Who Wanted Red Wings*
.   *The Ugly Duckling*
.   The Mad Hatter's Tea Party from *Alice in Wonderland*
.   Fables from Aesop and La Fontaine, such as "The City Mouse and the Country
    Mouse," and "The Tortoise and the Hare."
.   All the traditional tales concerning the magical three — — Three Little Pigs,
    Three Bears, Three Billy Goats Gruff, Three Little Kittens, etc.

If you take a story like *The Little Red Hen,* you realize two things:

.   The characters must be immediately recognizable, so a mask is a great help, and

.   The story involves a great deal of movement, so the simpler the mask, the
    better the mime. The Little Red Hen has to plant the wheat, reap it, take it
    to the mill, grind it into flour, and finally bake it into bread. In many versions
    of the story, the other lazy animals (the dog, the cat, the pig, etc.) while making
    their excuses, are "busy" doing other things, like splashing in mud, or gnawing
    on a bone. Masks will heighten these actions.

The Emperor's Nightingale (based on the story by Hans Christian Anderson)

The Chinese theatre has a tradition of masks and mime that is thousands of years old. Most libraries include at least one book on Chinese theatre, so investigate this ancient dramatic tradition and set your mime in Chinese style with a small band of musicians, playing cymbals, bells and gongs, seated on the side of the stage. They will make all your music and sound effects. On the other side of the stage you will need a venerable storyteller, and a Properties Person (very humble!)

In the original story a kitchen maid from the Royal Palace persuades the Nightingale to come and sing for the Emperor. Everyone takes pleasure in her beautiful voice, until the Emperor of Japan sends an elaborate artificial nightingale with a mechanical voice — — and the less ornamental real bird is forgotten. The exquisite gift is the talk of the Palace until one day it rattles and shakes its way to a standstill and cannot be fixed. All music is gone, the Emperor grows sick, and is on his deathbed when the true Nightingale returns to revive her master by singing outside his window.

You can expand the story to include may other birds in the forest. It will help to enforce a important theme in the original story: the Nightingale has much to lose when she leaves the forest to sing for the Emperor.

Anansi the Spider*

Anansi is a great hero to the people of West Africa — — half spider, half man. The legends of Anansi will provide you with an opportunity to work with fabulous African masks in glorious rich colors. The story of Anansi and his six spider sons (all with very different characteristics) is full of adventure and movement. Anansi is rescued from inside a fish (you might use at least four children to made one big fish); and from the beak of a falcon (two children can made a great swooping bird). At the end of the story Nyame the Sky God (if you have a beautiful authentic mask someone brought back from a visit to Africa, this is the moment to use it!) appears holding up the great white globe of the moon for all to see — — a prize for the six brave spider sons of Anansi.

The Twelve Labors of Hercules

For children of the Superhero Age, the twelve labors of Hercules are truly thrilling. I will not list all twelve adventures, as they may be found in any book on Greek mythology, but most of them concern terrifying beasts of one kind or another, and are very suitable for mime with masks. You can let your imagination run wild on these creatures. . .the masks can be as fantastical as the feats of Hercules himself. I would use animal noises and sound effects as the only accompaniment to these heroic deeds.

Noah's Ark

This story has captivated children over the centuries. I like to think of medieval children hearing the story and enjoying the action of the Mystery pageants. In fact the Bible is full of good actable stories, and some of the most appealing concern animals: Daniel in the lion's den, Jonah and the whale, Elijah being fed by the ravens, Adam and Eve and the serpent, and all the sheep and shepherd parables of the New Testament. All these stories lend themselves to animal masks.

Since I enjoyed working on Obey's play, *Noah,* I decided to expand the animal mime to other parts of the story not included in the Bible version. With fourth and fifth graders, in a summer program held out of doors, we mimed such scenes as

. the difficulties of finding two of each animal
. the problems of getting the animals into the ark
. the first time the lion and the lamb lay down together in the ark.
. the effect of wind and rain, and an enclosed space, for 40 days and 40 nights.
. the day the rain stopped.
. the parting of the ways, when the Ark reached land.

The children made very simple masks out of paper, and we acted out the story to a background of animal noises and folk music: "The Animals went in two by two — — hurrah, hurrah" and "Didn't it rain, Lord? Lord, didn't it rain!"

The Sea Serpent Chantey

This poem provides the occasion to make a vast long body mask for the Sea Serpent, using four to six people. I would put choral speakers on two platforms — — one, for the main verses of the poem; the other, to speak the chorus in ghostly undertones. The rest of the class would undulate through the gym or classroom, wherever you are doing it, as the Sea-Serpent. There is also a place for *mermaid* masks (bottom half of the body this time!) and your *pirates* may wear scarves or masks.

*There are many Anansi books; I have used *Anansi the Spider* by Gerald McDermott, Landmark Production, Inc., 1972.

There's a snake on the western wave
And his crest is red.
He is long as a city street,
And he eats the dead.
There's a hole in the bottom of the sea
Where the snake goes down.
And he waits in the bottom of the sea
For the men that drown.

Chorus
This is the voice of the sand
(The sailors understand)
"There is far more sea than sand,
There is far more sea than land.
    Yo. . .ho, yo. . .ho."

He waits by the door of his cave
While the ages moan.
He cracks the ribs of the ships
With his teeth of stone.
In his gizzard deep and long
Much treasure lies.
Oh, the pearls and the Spanish gold.
And the idols' eyes. . .
Oh, the totem poles. . .the skulls
The altars cold. . .
The wedding rings, the dice. . .
The buoy bells old.

Chorus

Die, mermaids, with sharp swords
And cut him through,
And bring us the idols' eyes
And the red gold too.
Lower the grappling hooks
Good pirate men
And drag him up by the tongue
From his deep wet den.
We will sail to the end of the world,
We will nail his hide
To the mainmast of the moon
In the evening tide.

(Repeat as a second chorus many times.)

Or will you let him live,
The deep-sea thing,
With the wrecks of all the world
In a black wide ring
By the hole in the bottom of the sea
Where the snake goes down,
Where he waits in the bottom of the sea
For the men that drown?
Chorus

by Vachel Lindsay

117 Animal Masks

Suppose the cast list for your play calls for

    Four Dandelions
    The Spirit of Spring
    Jack Frost
    The North Wind
    The Sun
    Two Clouds, and
    One Raindrop

Masks are obviously the answer to your costume dilemma. Abstract characterizations like these can only make one definitive statement, so this is the area where you can be most creative and experimental in your mask work.

Up till now I have spoken mostly of the "False *Face*" — or, at most, appendages like tails or paws or wings. Now we can sometimes ignore the face, and think of a mask to cover the entire body. In abstract mime, many of the characters you will be creating are faceless — like a Cloud, a Loaf of Bread, or Greed. You need to consider the shape and feeling you are trying to convey — and work this around the human body.

Materials

A whole range of materials can be used: huge sheets of paper, string, foam rubber, cardboard boxes, yards of stretch material, old sheets, left-over fabrics, plastic garbage

bags, old coats — even lamp shades! Just a word of caution, before you haul out that old TV carton from the attic. . .the first consideration in all mask work is still the movement. While a big box mask may make a big hit at the Fancy Dress Parade, the child wearing it may feel very restricted and uncomfortable.

Which Comes First — The Movement Or The Mask?

That depends. Sometimes a mask becomes the natural extension of a mime class. At other times the mask is made first, and the movement is dictated by the requirements of the mask (except, of course, the Neutral mask). Now that we are concerned with the possibility of the mask "taking over" the entire body, it is very important to decide the order of procedure.

Usually, in school plays with a cast list like the one at the beginning of this chapter, the schedule runs something like this:

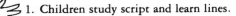

1. Children study script and learn lines.

2. Movement (if any!) is added.

3. Masks are made at the last minute (often by the mothers) and worn for the first time at Dress Rehearsal.

We are not concerned here with learning lines, but I do think that you find more creative mask-making if you have' worked first to develop the "feeling" of Sun, Wind, and Jack Frost in movement with the whole class. Then make the appropriate masks, and *then* read the script.

Nature Is A Stimulus To Abstract Mask-Making

The changing seasons are a constant and dramatic phenomenon, influencing all our lives, so it is no wonder that they get so much attention in both home and school. The weather and the elements have fascinated human beings for thousands of years. The Creation legends of Eskimos, Greeks, Aztecs, Norsemen and Africans all include abstract personifications of the Sun, the Moon, Night and Day, Thunder and Lightning.

To start, a good discussion of the weather brings out what we see and feel, and how we react at the different seasons of the year. With younger children, I like to read poems appropriate to the different seasons, and then mime different things that happen to plants, animals, birds and people in spring, summer, winter and fall. I include games, foods, chores, and above all the *feelings* that we have at these times. Then the mime might begin with Spring:

> You are the clouds that float across the sky on an April day, so full of moisture we know they will burst soon, and send down a shower of rain. Now you *are* that rain, falling through the sky, swirling through the gutter, rushing down the street, until you land in a big puddle and a little boy in new shoes comes and jumps right in the middle of you!
>
> Now, away from the city, high up in hills, you have been frozen all winter. Now, very slowly, you are warmed by the spring sunshine, penetrating the ice. It's breaking up, and trickling down the mountainside, flooding the valleys, pouring into the hard earth of winter and making it soft and wet and ready for planting.
>
> Way up in the sky lives the March Wind — a powerful force when he moves

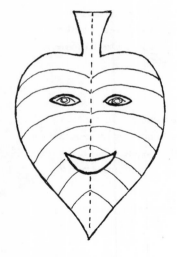

down closer to earth, shaking the bare trees, whistling down the chimneys, blowing off the scarecrow's hat, and making the wash dance on the clothesline.

You can repeat the same process with the other three seasons, then divide the group into four, giving each group a season. I let them choose their own list of characters. For Spring we might have a March Wind, April Showers, Rainbow, and Waterfall; for Summer, the hot Sun, Thunder, Lightning and a Forest Fire. Fall might include the Harvest Moon, a Breeze, and Falling Leaves, while Winter brings Snowflakes, Jack Frost, a Blizzard and Ice.

Some of the masks you make for these characters can be face masks; others cover the body. There is no reason why you may not use a combination of the two. Once your masks are made and you have experimented with appropriate movement, make a still-life picture of each season. To bring the scenes to life, play some music like Vivaldi's *The Seasons* or Beethoven's Pastoral Symphony.

Apart from the Seasons and the Elements, try fruits, flowers, vegetables, plants: the whole of Nature is mask-worthy. Collect poems, stories, and songs, then make appropriate masks, and do the mime while the song is sung or the story or poem is read. Here are some good ones:

. "The Little Christmas Tree," Hans Christian Anderson

. "The Sun and the Wind," Aesop

. "Dandelion, Dandelion, Yellow as Gold," Anonymou

. "Vegetables," Rae Lyman Field

. "Five Little Pumpkins," Anonymous

. "I'm a Lonely Little Petunia in an Onion Patch"

. "April Showers"

. "The North Wind Doth Blow"

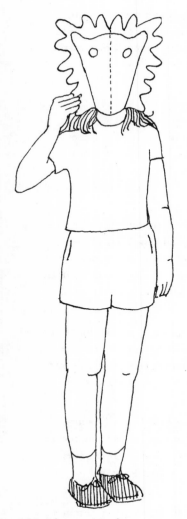

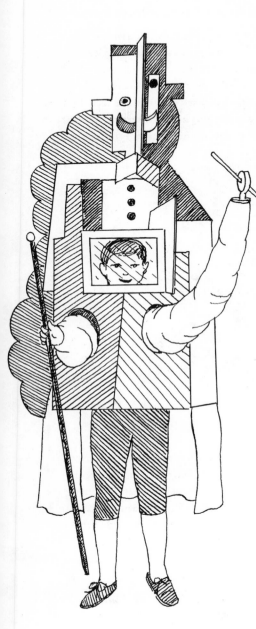

Masks For Abstract Characterizations

Beside the delightful, if somewhat hackneyed theme of the abstract personification of nature, we can introduce children to abstract ideas about *people,* based on feelings, characteristics, and ideas.

This Picasso design for the ballet "Parade" shows you the ultimate in crazy character masks. The concept is as abstract and as complicated as a child's drawing may sometimes seem!

A good introduction to abstract characters is to start with ideas about ourselves. Take a box large enough to fit over the child's head, and cut out a square on one side. The child's face (the face we all see) shows through this opening — but does that tell us *everything* about this person? Decorate the other three sides of the box with "the other faces of Bobby." Sometimes he's mad (turn the mask to show the angry Bobby); sometimes he is silly (turn the mask to show the silly side); sometimes he is dreamy (turn that part of his character out front).

In medieval times, many characters were abstractions like Greed, Lust, Good Deeds and Beauty. The characterizations were simple, with no development through the play. The good were good — the bad were bad. I once played the delightful role of Dame Chastity in a 15th century Scottish play, *The Three Estates.* I was tied in the stocks by "Lechery," "Lust," and "Lasciviousness"! Not suitable for your average kindergarten class — but it gave me the idea for a class on masks based on ideas the children could understand. We made character masks with paper bags featuring

. *Money* (the mask was covered in play money and we even discussed a story line where some money-crazy characters lived in a home were the furniture, drapes, clothes, *everything* literally said "Money!")

. *Greed* (a paper collage mask with cut-outs of food from magazines, pasted all over the mask)

. *Brainy* (the mask was an extra-large brain that fitted on top of the head like a hat, and was attached to a large pair of eyeglasses)

. *Nosy* — just an enormous nose, fitted around the ears — great for poking into everyone else's business!

. *TV Addict* (his mask was a TV set, with antennae and even a copy of TV Guide clipped to the side of the mask.)

. *Happiness* (the familiar yellow smile face)

. *Messy* (this mask was mostly a scribbly mess, with lots of wild-looking paper hair.)

We shared the masks, trying on the different characters one by one. I then put two or three characters into groups, and gave them a meeting place. . .a parking lot, an airplane, a movie theatre, a picnic ground. They improvised from there.

In cases like these, it is most definitely the mask that dictates the movement. The characters of the famous children's theatre group, the Paper Bag Players, are conditioned by the type and shape and decoration of the paper bag they are wearing. Abstract masks offer you the opportunity to experiment with all sorts of unusual materials. The Mummenshanz players use a toilet paper roll mask, shown as the frontispiece for this chapter, for all manner of communicating. As the toilet paper unravels, it appears that the mask is crying. . .sticking out its tongue in derision. . .laughing. . .

quarreling. Another Mummenshanz mask is made up of little note pads. With magic markers, the Mimes make eyes and mouth on the pads, conveying the whole range of human emotions, ripping off pages from the pads when they are ready to change features. I am sure a creative group of children would have great fun with these masks. Who hasn't wanted to fool around with yards of toilet-paper, and scribble on note pads!

Even if you do not feel you can invest in dozens of toilet paper rolls for masks, you *can* gather a large collection of scrap materials and fabrics — unusual papers, yarn and string. Make masks which concentrate on the *texture* of the material — rough. . . smooth. . .shiny. . .sticky. . .prickly. . .cool. . .velvety. Start with a "hands on. . . eyes closed" experience with the fabric, and then develop characters from the feel of the material. The interest here lies in exchanging masks and playing with several different characters, so the masks should be simple enough — and strong enough — for easy exchange.

With small children, you — or the children — can narrate a simple story while the children mime the action. For example —

> Once upon a time a warm-hearted girl called Velvety Violet came purring down the street, when who should come along but Prickly Peter, the most difficult guy in the world. Catastrophe! Poor Violet just could not get away. The more she tried, the more entangled she became. Fortunately Slippery Sam happened to come sliding past, and he finally managed to slide between the two of them and free poor Violet. Violet and Sam became *very* friendly, until Wet-look Wendy arrived — skating. Slippery Sam loves to skate — and Violet was afraid to get wet. . .

Another kind of abstract character mask can be based on the *Signs of the Zodiac*. Many people consider that one's fate or personality is dictated by the date of his birth — and almost everyone is interested in this very abstract idea. "When were you born?" I ask my older classes. "What is your sign of the Zodiac?" I bring along a book describing the various characteristics of the different signs, and then send everyone away to make masks to show the temperament that goes with their sign. . .Aquarius. . . Scorpio. . .Libra.

I like to start with a masked entrance through curtains or from behind a screen, and then say, "Do something that shows us what kind of personality you are." You can then put opposing Signs of the Zodiac into some taxing situation, such as having Capricorn and Pisces in a rowboat when a terrible storm comes up.

Abstract Masks Based On Man-Made Objects

Again, the idea of being "a thing" appeals greatly to children. Large cardboard boxes can be worn on the body and can readily convert a boy or girl into a washing machine, a clock radio, or a computer. Smaller masks can be made out of all sorts of materials, like this marvelous "Money" mask, made by an 8-year-old boy and worn with the cryptic comment, "My father should wear this — that's all he ever thinks about!"

The whole class can work on a creative project with abstract body masks, like *Kaleidescope*. Most children own these magical toys, so ask the children to bring in and share their kaleidescopes. Discuss the shapes, colors and patterns, and the way they quickly move and change. Then make facial or body masks from colorful paper in a great variety of shapes (a good project to do with the art teacher). Now you have a feast of color; put on some rich, colorful music like the Carousel Waltz from the Rodgers and Hammerstein musical, and let the children become kaleidescopes. The change of pattern has a definite rhythm — and if you are fortunate enough to have a room with mirrors to work in, you can make something quite beautiful.

A similar project, perhaps for a Fourth of July holiday, is a *Fireworks Display.* Think of the way a skyrocket, a Roman Candle, a Catherine Wheel and a firecracker move, and you will see that this is a wonderful opportunity for extravagant and inventive movement. Try accompanying it with Stravinsky's Fireworks Fantasy.

Another mime especially suited to body masks is based on *Games.* Ask the children to bring in their favorite board games — checkers, Scrabble, chess, Bingo, cards, etc. Now, working with large sheets of paper, make body masks like sandwich boards for the different game pieces. You might turn your gymnasium into a large-scale Giants' Casino, and invite another class (the Giants) to come and play with these big Dice, Chess pieces, Playing Cards and Dominos. The movement will naturally be stiff, like robots, so this is a good project to follow a lesson on machines and mechanical movement.

The Ultimate Body Mask — The Stretch Bag

The stretch bag serves as a wonderful introduction to the world of ghosts — and the use of large fabric masks like old sheets or pillow cases. It should be made of some stretchy material like jersey, and can be painted and decorated, or left plain. Sew together the two long sides of the fabric, leaving both ends of the "tube" free. This allows for more than one child to get into the tube — which is always great fun.

Put on some music with a strong beat — rhythm blues, rock and roll, jazz. The bodies inside the stretch bag will respond accordingly. A rhythm band will also provide an interesting beat, and so will a collection of sound effects. You will want to experiment with slow and fast movements and ultimately with the use of silence.

Jersey is not a cheap fabric, so you will probably only use one or two stretch masks at a time. But these are so fascinating to watch that you need never fear that the other children will become bored awaiting their turn.

An older group may be ready for one of the most famous mime plays of this century: Samuel Beckett's *Act Without Words No. III.* In this play, two characters, "A" and "B," are discovered in two sacks (or stretch bags) on a bare stage. They are inert until a goad (a long pole) pokes "A" into action, and he enacts a day's work, rhythmically punctuated by meditation, when he retires to his sack. The goad comes from the wings again, and this time pokes the sack containing "B." "B" jumps to life and briskly goes through his daily round, this time punctuated by the constant consultation of his watch.

My own feeling is that Beckett is trying to tell us about two modes of life: one distinctly Eastern, or philosophical; the other very Western and mechanized. The play is highly effective with Junior High students and makes an excellent extension of the Stretch Bag mask-work.

Ghost Masks

Another place to go after all the fun of the stretch bags is *Ghosts.* Use old sheets with eyes cut out and some means of securing the sheet to the hands. Here we are working with another kind of body mask — this one free-flowing and floating.

"Do you believe in ghosts?" That is a question that never fails to get a response at all age levels. If you can drag them away from discussing this fascinating topic *before* you have brought in your sheet masks), put on some spooky music, or a fearsome sound-effects record, and take a trip to a haunted house to look for ghosts and put everyone in the mood!

> Down the rickety path, past the hissing black cat with the arched back, and knock at the big black door. Suddenly, mysteriously, it swings open to reveal a hallway full of dusty old statues. Push your way through the spider webs and climb the creaking staircase, until you reach that long black windy corridor which leads to *the* room. In *that* room is a big dark closet, and in that closet is. . .THE GHOST!

After all the excitement, sit down and discuss the kind of ghost who lives in a closet. Is it friendly. . .scary. . .old. . .young? Is it on a special mission to haunt someone, like the ghosts in Dickens' *Christmas Carol?* Who knows some really good ghost stories?

I ask the children to bring me in *one* of the following:

. A good ghost story;
. Some ghostly sound effects, or music;
. Some old white sheets — or anything else suitable to make ghost-masks;
. Some lighting effects like candles or flashlights to add to the effect.

One group of children narrates their own stories, while another group acts them out, wearing the ghost masks, and a third group adds the sound effects. One or two children can be in charge of the lighting arrangements. A great deal of fun!

The Masque of the Yellow Fever

Finally, I would like to share with you the story of the most successful mask-lesson I have ever taught. This was done in a summer drama program with children from 8 to 14 in Watts, Los Angeles, in 1967. (1966, if you remember, was the summer of the riots, so one of the purposes of this drama program was to give the children a positive and creative experience, and prevent another wild, hot, destructive summer.)

It all began when I asked the children to make masks — any mask — at home, and bring them to the school where I was working. I shall never forget the sixth grade boy who hissed his way insidiously around the corner of the classroom door, wearing a terrifying "Yellow Fever" mask, and then headed straight in my direction, the hissing sound growing louder and louder all the time! When he touched me, I was truly terrified.

Many primitive people have been wiped off the face of the earth through "civilized" diseases. Even chicken pox could be deadly to an Indian tribe. In medieval times, the mask of death (a skeleton mask) often danced through the streets as a sign that the plague, or some other dread disease, was on its way. Nowadays, when I hear of someone who has one of our modern diseases, like cancer or diabetes, it almost seems as if a masked figure has reached down and taken possession of that body.

I told the boy that his mask looked like yellow fever, and we discussed all we could about this disease, and the horrors it caused during the building of the Panama Canal. We decided to set our play in an African village. The men went out to hunt. . .the women ground corn, the children played the drums. Suddenly a messenger came in from another village to announce the news — disease was coming! Immediately the drummer changed his happy tune to one full of menace, and the tale of approaching danger. The men left their hunting, and the women gathered up the children, but even as they did so the hissing sounds of "The Disease" could be heard in the distance.

The children had made five more yellow fever masks (simple facial masks of thick paper spattered with red) and one by one each of the masked figures crept, or crawled, or jumped, or slid into the village and touched their victims. The villagers shook with the high fever, their bones ached, and eventually, writing in agony, they all dropped to the floor while the masked figures stood triumphantly over them.

Now six other figures, half-masked in white, came on the scene, carrying vaccine, syringes, medicine bottles, and other such hygenic weapons. A life-and-death battle ensued, until one by one the Disease masks faltered and died. As the last "Disease" died, the doctors and nurses ripped off their white surgical masks, and the people all celebrated with a dance.

This mime was done without music except for a drum, and "utterance" — humming, whistling, happy sounds at the beginning, the hissing sound of the Yellow Fever, growing louder and more persistent. The doctors and nurses made no sound, until the last hiss of the disease had faded away, when a great shout of joy went up, and the drums were played for the final dance of celebration.

Children love being in a performance. Think back to your own school days. Can you remember the details of your math or spelling lessons? Now, can you remember being in the school play? I am *sure* the answer to the second question is "YES!" Every child needs a special occasion for which to dress up and perform — at least once in a lifetime.

Most teachers choose a scripted play for such an occasion. They feel safe with that solid print and all the directions at hand. And here are *words* — words to be read and memorized; no one can accuse them of getting away from the basics!

So what is wrong with using a script? Nothing. . .*if* it is good exciting material written in a natural style with believable well-drawn characters. . .*if* the children all have the ability to read well and memorize their lines. . .*if* it provides satisfying parts for all the children in the group, so that you can avoid creating a "star system" at an early age.

Consider the mime play. It poses none of the problems just listed and, most important, it provides the opportunity for all the children to display something they do well — mime!

Audiences have been surprised at just how creative and how entertaining a mime play can be. It is also ideal entertainment for all ages to watch, from the pre-school sister or brother to the 85-year-old great grandmother who has never spoken very much English. Everyone can enjoy mime.

The Mime play can also be custom-built to suit the needs and talents of your particular group. You can add or subtract characters. . .include hard-of-hearing or other special-education children who would be hard to incorporate into a scripted play. . .capitalize on the talents of children who are good at acrobatics, dancing, clowning, music or sound effects.

Where Will You Perform?

The first thing I consider is the available space. A classroom. . .an all purpose room. . .gym. . .a large or small platform stage? Or out of doors? As a general rule, if you have limited space, you should limit crowd scenes. Perhaps you'll develop a series of small scenes with only one or two characters in each one. If you have a small platform-style stage with very little wing space, consider a play using frontal masks, or else sit the audience on stage, and use the floor of the hall for your performance. Remember to use as many interesting places for entrances and exits as you can — a procession through the audience can be very effective.

If you are performing in a large open space, remember that there are many different

ways for your audience to be seated (and you don't *have* to seat them — in *Pictures at an Exhibition* the audience moves around the room with the players.)

The Rehearsal Process

Many mime plays develop naturally from a successful series of lessons. Or you may have a particular story you want to use. Either way, the rehearsal process for a mime play is a little different than for a play with words. As you prepare your scenario, you will be thinking

. What is the purpose of the story — to entertain, to bring a message, to involve the audience emotionally, to make them laugh?

. How can it best be done in the available space?

. What other visual effects will enhance the story: make-up, masks, scenery of any kind, costumes, lighting effects?

I find the best way to try out for parts in a mime play is for everyone to try out at once for the most important roles. For example, if you need an Old Woman, as in "I Knew an Old Lady Who Swallowed a Fly," let everyone — boys and girls — join in miming the Old Lady. As you survey the class, jot down the names of likely candidates.

Of course, if the play you are doing has evolved from a mime class, you will probably remember children who were particularly adept in certain roles. One of the joys of mime plays is that, unlike a scripted play, you don't necessarily have to cast your best readers in the most important parts.

It is essential that the movement in a mime play be carefully rehearsed. Being creative should not be an excuse for chaos — especially in performance! By the time of performance, everyone must know exactly when and where to enter, how and where to move, and make his exit. While it is true that most mime plays do not need as much rehearsal time as the scripted play, since you are not concerned with lines and blocking, projecting the voice, and interpreting the words, movement must also "speak" — with clarity and imagination.

What Accompanies Your Story — Music. . .Narration. . .Sound Effects?

Sometimes music itself can be the inspiration for a mime play. With experienced children, you may only need to play some stimulating music to be rewarded with an original story line and theme. If, on the other hand, you are going to develop the mime play first, and then look for accompanying music, you have quite a task before you. I have suggested music for different mime lessons, and for some of the plays, but it often takes quite a search to find something which is appropriate and the right length for the action in your play.

Use live music if you possibly can. I like to experiment with as many musical instruments as possible — recorders, flutes, drums, whistles, guitars, piano, whatever — all can play an important role in setting the mood for a mime play. Encourage the children to play their own music. On one very successful occasion, I worked with the music teacher. Quite simply, I showed her the action of the play, and asked her to direct the children in providing the music. The result was a highly successful marriage of our two complementary art forms.

Sound effects and "utterance" can be equally effective in other plays. You may consider having a Sound Effects Band, who sit on the side of the stage, as in the Chinese theatre, or you may want to let the mime players themselves make their own sound effects.

For many plays — many mime lessons — the best and most eloquent accompaniment is

SILENCE

Do not be afraid to use it. It need not be an empty awkwardness, but a meaningful, dynamic, and poignant part of the play.

Properties

There are no hard and fast rules. You may wish to use —

. No properties whatsoever. Everything is mimed. It becomes particularly important to make sure your occupational mime is clean and clear and believable.

. A few representative and essential properties which add style — and perhaps comic variation. All properties should be in the same style. If you have only a few of them, they will be very conspicuous; make them look good.

. All real properties, and perhaps complete costumes and scenery. The famous mime play "L'Enfant Prodigue," with music by Wormser, uses complete sets, costumes. and properties. In fact it uses everything you would expect to find in a natural-istic production of a scripted play — except words. So a very naturalistic mime play might require a full complement of real props.

Costumes

If you are using masks, in most cases, the mask is your costume. Most facial masks work best with the simplest clothes — leotard, solid-colored pants and shirt, even blue jeans. Nothing should distract from the focal point of the mask.

In a mime play without masks, costume of any kind is an important part of the visual effect. As a general rule, what looks good in a photograph or a film will also look good in a mime play. Bold, primary colors, stripes, exaggerated outline and enlarged detail all make a clear, immediate statement on stage. Look at the costumes worn by the stock characters of the Commedia dell' Arte. They were designed to rivet every eye in the large crowds in the piazza when the player entered the little platform stage.

If you have ever wondered why famous mimes like Marcel Marceau tend to wear plain pants and striped T-shirts — it is because they look good, and can be seen from the back of the audience with ease.

Make-Up

Some make-up — like the witch or clown's — is so complete that it can be considered a mask. If, however, you are not using masks, and would simply like to add character or style with make-up, you must be guided by the overall visual effect. An exaggerated,

stylized form of make-up may work quite well in fantasy mime plays. Make-up for ballet has always been more stylized than for the theatre. Since mime belongs somewhere between the two art forms, you can move in either direction: stylized or natural. Many plays in the round, where the audience is very close, will do better with little or no make-up.

If you have two or three different helpers applying the make-up, make sure they all know the style you have chosen. Otherwise you can end up with one child looking as if he were performing in a 19th century ballet, while the next one is ready for Halloween, and yet a third has so little on you are not even sure he has been "done!"

If you are using stage lights, survey the make-up under your lights . . . red gelatins, for example, can change the effect of make-up completely.

Lighting

If you are fortunate enough to work in a space with adequate lighting facilities, then a mime play is your opportunity for a "Field Day."

You have no script to supply lighting cues, so it is essential that whoever is operating your lighting comes to several rehearsals and familiarizes himself thoroughly with the action. As director you should provide the lighting people with a scenario of the action well in advance — and also a tape of the music or sound effects. I once directed a mime play which evolved from the overture of Rossini's *The Barber of Seville*. For that 8-minute piece of very busy music, there were nearly 50 lighting cues!! Wonderful exercise for the teenage lighting technician.

Scenery

I have purposely left this to last, because my feeling about scenery for mime plays is that you should not use it. Mime is concerned with the movement of bodies in space Just as a good photograph is set off by an uncluttered background, so a mime play makes its best statement against a plain curtain. A great deal of busy painted flats will only attract the eye away from the mime.

Like all rules in the theatre, this one can be broken with stunning results, but for most plays, scenery should be confined to the creation of different levels. Think in terms of creating visual variety by the use of ladders, platforms, gym risers, tables, screens, blackboards, desks and stools.

In the mime plays that follow, the focus is on the kinetic expression of the children rather than on the scenery. They will give you an example of what has worked well in performance. I hope some of you may enjoy doing them — or at least, that they will stimulate you to seek your own mime plays to perform.

I KNOW AN OLD LADY WHO SWALLOWED A FLY

A mime play based on the song — suitable for K-2nd grade

CAST

Old Lady (no mask)

Animals   **Fly**

                         Spider

                         Bird

                         Cat

                         Dog

                         Goat

                         Cow

                         Horse

1 Mouth (2 Children) — see picture

All animals are masked, some with body masks like the spider. Think also of adding other animal effect, like a tail for the cow, paws for the cat, or wings for the bird.

PROPS

1 Fly Swatter	A Small Hedge
1 Dog Leash	1 3-legged Milking Stool
1 Bone	1 Horse's Bridle

MUSIC

The music is played by a rhythm band seated at one side of the stage. On the opposite side of the stage there is a chorus of singers who sing the song "I Know An Old Lady Who Swallowed A Fly." Everytime an animal is mentioned in the song — it is accompanied by a specific musical instrument.

Fly — *Triangle*
Spider — *Maracas*
Bird — *Bells*
Cat — *Sticks*
Dog — *Wood Blocks*

Goat — *Tamborine*
Cow — *Xylophone*
Horse — *Coconut Shells*
After "she died, of course" — *Cymbal*

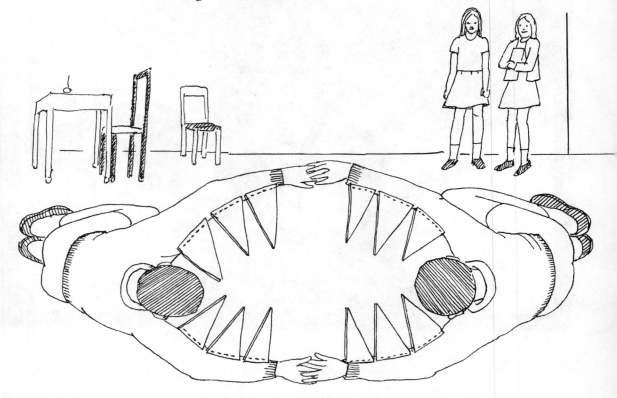

As an introduction to working on this play, everyone should learn to sing this song. It is important for all the children to know the exact order of animals swallowed by the Old Lady. Some practice in fainting dead is a good idea too, as the Old Lady has to die dramatically at the end of the play. Young children are so relaxed, they usually fall easily, but it is worthwhile doing it the right way. In what direction would she fall — backwards, frontwards, sideways? Make sure there is room for the fall. Remember one principle for all stage falls:

Kneel
Sit
Lie

If you leave out any part of this formula, you can fall on some uncomfortable part of the anatomy like the nose, the elbow, the knee. It is much better to use a well-cushioned part like the behind. Before any fall there is an impetus — the breath taken in — as the arrow pierces the skin, or the punch on the jaw is felt. In this play the Old Lady should suddenly clutch her stomach and then fall flat — a very "hammy" fall.

When children fall as a matter of course in the middle of a mime lesson, it is usually no cause for concern, but the tension suggested by the fall in a play — with audience watching — can create problems. So, have a falling session first with the whole group participating. For fun, let everyone take turns to ENTER AND DIE!! Everyone loves to do this, and you can have a great variety of falls: poisoning, gunshots, arrows, fainting, knives and for further inspiration, refer to any TV program from 8 P.M. onwards.

To cast the play I would suggest you try animal mime first with everyone becoming a fly, a spider, bird, cat and so forth. For the Old Lady refer to Chapter IV, Page 29, and remember the Old Lady must sustain her character and her age throughout the play.

SCENARIO

Enter an Old Lady. She looks around her imaginary kitchen and opens closets and her refrigerator. Everything is empty. She says (in mime) "I am so hungry." (Throughout all this the chorus hums the tune of "I Know An Old Lady Who Swallowed A Fly.) Suddenly a Fly comes buzzing on stage — the Old Lady has an idea! She fetches a fly swatter and chases the Fly all over the stage trying to catch it. A Spider jumps out and catches the Fly in his web. The Old Lady is scared of spiders, but she is so hungry! So she wrestles with the Spider for the Fly and the song begins. She drags the Fly over to The Mouth and swallows the Fly. The Mouth closes snap! Meanwhile the Spider is laughing like crazy, the body heaving up and down. The Old Lady has another idea and she repeats in mime "I feel hungry." A different kind of chase ensues (the Fly buzzed all over the place). The Spider is lured into The Mouth as the Old Lady repeats the eating process and a second verse of the song is sung. Enter the Bird. She flies around and then hops about looking for bird seed. The Old Lady fetches some crumbs and tricks the bird into coming to her. She admires the beautiful feathers. The Bird whistles and sings until the Old Lady has another idea! Repeat the swallowing process with The Mouth. The Cat enters looking everywhere for the Bird. The Dog enters from the other side of the stage. The two meet. The Cat arches her back and hisses and the dog growls. They circle one another until at last they fight. The Old Lady separates them and lectures them on fighting. She does "a nice pussy routine" with the Cat and lures her into The Mouth. The Dog sees what has happened and tries to escape, but the Old Lady catches him. She pets him, puts him on a leash and takes him for a walk. He forgets all about the Cat. The Old Lady entices him with a bone until he too is drawn into The Mouth. Enter Goat in silly goat fashion. The Goat bleats and the Old Lady says "I'm still hungry". The Old Lady goes off-stage and brings in a little hedge which she carries over to the Goat like a camouflage. The Goat nibbles on it and gets his horns stuck — and the hedge and the Goat are pulled over to The Mouth. The Old Lady tries tasting a bite of the Goat. Too tough! She swallows him anyway, but has terrible indigestion. The Cow enters. She needs to be milked. The Old Lady fetches a milking stool and starts to milk the Cow. The Cow is very happy until the Old Lady suddenly says "I am *still* hungry!" The Cow suffers the same fate as the rest of the animals. The Horse comes in. He paws the ground, and the Old Lady fetches a bridle, puts it on the Horse, and he takes her for a ride on his back. She gives him sugar. Kisses him. And boots him into The Mouth! The last line of the song is sung as the Old Lady dies a spectacular death!

For a curtain call, all the animals come out of The Mouth and dance around the prostrate figure of the Old Lady. The Horse goes over to The Mouth and shuts it very firmly. The Old Lady comes alive to take her bow.

"PICTURES AT AN EXHIBITION"

A mime without masks to be done to a recording of the Moussorgsky/Ravel music, for upper elementary children

CAST

Russian family — children and adults (four or five)

Picture No. 1	Gnome	Picture No. 5	Three Chicks
	Gnome's Victim — a scared creature		Mother Hen
Picture No. 2	Two Ghosts	Picture No. 6	One Rich Old Fat Jewish Man
	A Knight in Armour		One Poor Beggar
	Spider	Picture No. 7	Market Sellers and Buyers
Picture No. 3	Two Nannies (Nurse-maids)	Picture No. 8	Two or Three Skeletons
	Four Children	Picture No. 9	Baba Yaga — the witch
Picture No. 4	Ox		A Chicken Hut — made of people
	Farmer	Picture No. 10	The Great Gate of Kiev — everyone

All properties are mimed.

Costumes should be in 19th Century style.

This mime is suitable for production in either of two styles:

On a proscenium stage, in which case each picture in the exhibit is presented on stage, and the "Promenade" — the procession of the Russian family walking through the exhibition — goes through the audience to view the pictures, displayed in the vast frame of the proscenium arch.

In the round, using a gym, hall, or all-purpose room as your exhibition hall. In this case the audience will promenade with the Russian family from one picture to the next. In this format, the pictures will be on exhibition as still lifes, each in their separate frames. When their music is played and the Promenade reaches them, they come to life. At the end of the movement they jump back in their frame, as they were at the beginning.

Sometimes there is Promenade music between one picture and another; sometimes one picture leads directly into the next. Where there is a Promenade, follow the mood the music suggests. The music after the Catacombs is soft and spooky as the family creeps away, a little scared by the picture. In the final Great Gate of Kiev, a grand Promenade with all the audience is definitely called for, no matter which staging you use.

Do not look at the original pictures which inspired the music. They are rather dull little etchings, and the Moussourgsky/Ravel music is far superior. Of course you may interpret the music any way you wish for your exhibition — but I have taken the titles of the Pictures, listened carefully to the music with a group of children, and I give you their suggestions for the come-to-life pictures.

SCENARIO

Promenade begins the procession through the exhibition with the family, collecting guides, — paying entrance fees — there is some misbehavior, and admonitions for the younger members. Glasses are adjusted, cameras left at the door and if you are doing it in the round, the audience is collected and taken to the first picture.

You will easily distinguish the beginning of each picture in the music.

1. THE GNOME

A strange hunch backed little creature suddenly springs to life and fetches a pot, and ingredients for his spell. He drops them, one by one into his pot. He does a crazy little dance around the pot — tastes the magic brew and offers some to the audience. He then drags in his first victim (who was crouching in a corner) to drink from the pot. He laughs when the victim turns into a frog — a spider — a snake and finally a monster! The gnome has been too clever! The monster overpowers the gnome, pushes him into "his" corner, takes his hat and resumes the same position as the gnome for the end of the music.

2. THE OLD CASTLE

It is inhabited by 2 ghosts, a spider, and a knight in armor. The knight and spider are already in position — The 2 ghosts suddenly come to life; they push through spider webs — until they come to a winding staircase. They go up and around up and around — and they invite one of the children from the family to explore the castle with them. They hand him a flashlight, and they travel through the castle until they reach the knight in armor. The spider suddenly wakes up and is angry that he is disturbed. He scurries around the castle; the ghost hides and the child is scared stiff and shines a light on the armor. One part moves. . .one hand. . .one arm and gradually, like the tin man, it begins to walk — right out into the audience. The spider tries to get it back — but it keeps on going. The two ghosts flit in front of it — and with spooky hands make it go backwards into the picture. The spider, the child and the two ghosts dance around the armor. A clock strikes 6 and the child is pushed out of the picture because the others have to resume their original positions.

3. TUILERIES GARDENS — A PARK IN PARIS

You can hear the children calling "NA NA" in the music. 4 children and 2 old fashioned Nannies knitting and talking while their charges play ball — hopscotch — leap frog — swing — slide — pick flowers — fall down — fight, and whatever else you have time for in the music.

4. BYLDO — THE OLD POLISH OX CART

Very heavily laden with hay, the cart goes up a hill and then way on down the road. If you are doing this in the round, let the ox cart go in and out of the picture, into the center of the room (the hill), dump the load and come back. An old farmer is busy at the beginning loading hay onto his (imaginary) ox cart. The ox is anxious to be going, and he has trouble keeping the ox in harness. At last he is ready to go. The poor old ox struggles up an imaginary hill — and even has to be pushed from behind by the farmer — at last they reach their destination. The farmer has a drink and gives some water to the ox. He unloads his hay, and they set off again until they "freeze" into the picture.

5. THE BALLET OF THE CHICKS

This delightful music was written for the Russian ballet school children — and the picture in the exhibition is actually the costume design for the ballet. 3 little chicks are curled up in their eggs — until they peck their way through the shell to the world outside. Enter mother — very proud of her brood — she offers each one a worm and makes them dance for her. They all fight for food on the ground. Mother hen makes them stretch their wings and flap them about — then she scurries out of the picture while they do a comical dance.

6. TWO OLD POLISH JEWS

The characters are very clearly defined in the music. Enter a very fat rich man with a big watch which he consults. He sits at a table and takes out a big box of money. He puts on his glasses, and starts to count the money, and drinks his vodka and eats cake. Enter the wheedling thin old begger. He sidles up to the table and begs a few crumbs of cake. He gets a little — and is told to go away. He comes back, and begs some vodka. At last the rich old man gives him some. He goes away — he comes back again and begs money. He sits at a table pulling up a stool and with fingers creeping across the table (he wears old wool gloves with no fingers) he tries to steal money. Rich man gives him a big argument. The begger says "just one little coin" and so it goes on. In the end the rich man throws the whole box at him and stomps away in disgust.

7. LIMOGES MARKET

The music gives a bustling busy effect. Decide what is sold at your market. Have people weighing, selling and buying — trying on clothes — eating — tasting. Use as many children as possible for this old-fashioned open-air market. Have one interesting event like a child tipping over a basket of fruit and being chased by the stall owner through the market (or through the audience).

8. CATACOMBS

This is very scary music. If you can make some skeleton costumes (two or three) and let them come to life and dance through the audience, that would be fun. The music is not very long, as it is followed by a long scared promenade, while the audience and family creeps towards —

9. BABA YAGA

Baba Yaga, the Russia witch, first seen on her broomstick, suddenly comes to life, and "flies" through the audience collecting human bones, ears, noses, hands, feet, so she can grind them up in her mortar and pestle. She lives in a hut on chicken legs. If you could make such a hut (with other children wearing chicken feet, or as an art project), Baba Yaga can whoosh in and out of her house, while making her "people-pie."

10. GREAT GATE OF KIEV

A huge procession. Gather up everything you can think of for use in a parade, flags, banners, incense, robes with long trains, "pretend" musical instruments, floats, gowns, hats, batons. Distribute them to the audience. Russian family will organize everyone in the audience to follow them with the music all the way around the room and up onto the stage or else out through your own doors which are now transformed into the Great Gate of Kiev. Music is quite long, so you have plenty of time during the first part (before the Promenade tune begins) to get the audience dressed in their Parade stuff. Procession can have a Russian character, if you wish, or else you can make it any visiting procession to go through the Great Gate of Kiev.

"THE WAR MACHINE"

A mime play with masks for older grades

This mime is based on several different ideas. I was very inspired by the Joffrey Ballet's dance drama "The Green Table". Here the actors wear masks and enact a story about war, and the meetings around the Green Peace Table. The first verse of this Bob Dylan poem was another influence.

> Come you masters of war,
> That build all the guns
> You that build the death planes
> And the big bombs.
> You that hide behind walls—
> You that hide behind desks—
> I just want you to know
> I can see through your masks.

The third influence was a group of grade six boys, working on machine mimes who developed a terrifying "War Machine" — comprising machine guns, ballistic missiles, atomic warheads, and a robot who sat in the middle of the whole machine, ready to let off the nuclear device.

This mime could be adapted for use with a mixed group of boys and girls. At the time, I was looking for something that would appeal to the energy of a group of boys who found any excuse to turn the class into a free-for-all fight. This served the purpose. They wanted a play that used: 1. fights 2. machines 3. masks 4. lots of action 5. some funny parts.

This play can be done "in the round" or on a regular stage.

CAST

Six fighting members of the Red Country wearing red masks
Six Red War Machine Parts (all form one large machine)

Six fighting members for the Blue Country wearing blue masks
Six Blue War Machine Parts (all form one large machine)

Two White-Faced Clowns (neutrals)

Suggested accompaniment: "Mars; The Bringer of Wars" from "The Planet Suite" by Gustav Holst

PROPERTIES

One long white ribbon
Six pairs of plastic knives and forks in red
Six pairs of plastic knives and forks in blue
Two toy swords

COSTUMES

Shirt and tie for the members of each country
and simple half-masks in red and blue

The Clowns should wear white loose fitting shirts,
black pants and white make-up.
The War Machine should be dressed in red or blue leotards and tights. They wear no masks until the Clowns bring in the funny masks made to look as crazy as possible, in bright colors and decorated with party favors.

At the opening scene there are two groups, the Red Masks and the Blue Masks, pounding on the table and arguing in mime. Some of them walk away from the table in disgust. The Red Side spells out three conditions. The Blue Side says no. The negotiations go back and forth until everyone is very excited. At last two White Faced "make-up" Clowns enter. They are neutral. They fool around lying on the table and finally they take away the table and bring a large piece of white ribbon on the stage. The Clowns send the Blue Masks to one side of the stage, the Reds to the other. They divide the space in half and sit holding the white ribbon like guards at the border between two countries. The Blues and the Reds sit down to eat. One member on each side brings in an imaginary roast beef (or pie) and plastic knives and forks, enough for each member. The chief serves the food and they all eat in mime. While they are eating the Clowns grow tired of holding up the border line, they yawn and stretch out to go to sleep. In the Red Country one member notices this, sneaks away from the meal and moves the ribbon a little further to this side. (This way the Reds have more land.) The Blue Side notices the same thing and one member of the Blues sneaks out and changes it back again. Now two Reds put it back to their side, then two Blues — until suddenly the Clowns wake up, the two Sides are already at war but only with plastic knives and forks! A battle takes place, with the Clowns trying desperately to keep the peace between the two waring factions. At last they put down their knives and forks and the two leaders go off stage and fetch toy swords. They use them like Japanese sword fighters (use two boys in your group who have experience in Karate). At a crucial moment in the battle, the clowns come between the two leaders and manage to persuade them to withdraw. Each side goes into a huddle with their leaders while the Clowns straighten out the border line and sit there hopefully on guard. Eventually the huddles break up and the Reds and the Blues each exit and return bringing the different parts of their deadly War Machines. Each group builds an identical Machine on opposite sides of the stage. At this point the music stops but the Machines themselves repeat these words over and over again like sound effects:

> Nuclear Warhead
> Carbine Rifles
> Torpedoes
> Bazooka Rocket
> Heavy Guns
> Big Bomb

The Machines are gradually built and the sounds get louder and louder. The leaders switch off the machines. There is a moment of silence and then the Machines are turned to face one another across the border line. The Clowns are scared stiff! The two leaders move the Machines close to the border line and then both Reds and Blues depart to the back of the Machines to sleep. The lights dim. The two Clowns creep way down stage (if you have a spotlight you can follow their actions; if not let the Clowns use flashlights). They decide to dismantle the Machines. Very quietly they creep back to the Machines and slowly they take apart each Machine until they get to the very last part. An alarm sounds off. Both sides, the Reds and the Blues, wake up, the leaders retrieve their swords, they capture the Clowns and put them back to back with hands above heads by the border line. Slowly the Reds and the Blues circle the Clowns until each side has changed territory. While the leaders guard the Clowns the other members of each group examine the "dead Machines". The clowns begin to laugh. The Reds and the Blues look up scared. They realize they both look the same and very slowly one by one, alternating sides, they remove their masks and drop them on the floor. The Clowns cheer! They take the white border ribbon and tie up the two sides in one big happy circle. Now the Clowns decide to resurrect the Machines but first they go off stage and bring a collection of crazy funny masks. The masks have flowers on them and kazoos and party favors! The Clowns rebuild the Machines but now with the new masks the Machines say:

> I Love You
> Let's Have Fun
> Make Love, Not War
> Have a Candy
> Have Some Kisses
> Let's Have a Party!

The Clowns untie the Reds and the Blues and everyone has a party.

HOW THE WORLD WAS MADE
(According to Cheyenne Legend)

A mime play with narrated story, using masks and music, suitable for grades 3 to 5.

CAST

Narrator	Deer
Maheo (All Spirit)	Porcupine
Man	Horse
Woman	Buffalo
Fish	Spirit of Water
Crab	Spirit of Light
Crawfish	Spirit of Trees
Snowgoose	Spirit of Grass
Mallard	Spirit of Flowers
Coot	Spirit of Fruit
Turtle	Musician (One or two drums; flute)

Every civilization and religion has its own version of "How the World Was Made," and this particular Cheyenne legend shows clearly a people who understand a heritage of both Water (the Great Lakes region) and Earth (the Plains of the midwest). When I worked with Cree children in northwestern Ontario, I found that they had an uncanny feeling for wildlife, so their mime was both accurate and inspired. I wish I had known this story at that time, because I know they would have enjoyed acting it.

There are two requisites before you start working on this story —

1. Some studies on Indian life and history. . .particularly the life of the Plains Indians, like the Cheyenne. This should include study of the Buffalo, and its importance in the lives of the Cheyenne people. A good book which describes the masks and artifacts of the Indian people is *They Put on Masks*, by Byrd Baylor (Scribner's). This play could easily be the culmination of a study unit on Indians.

2. Work on animal mime is essential.

I suggest all the characters in the story be masked except the Man and Woman, who wear Indian costume. Remember that the masked characters have a great deal of movement, so the masks must be made to fit comfortably and move easily.

"How the World Was Made" works well in a gym or all-purpose room, with the audience seated all around. The entire story is read by the narrator, leaving all the animals, birds and spirits free to interpret the story through movement. Your narrator reads the story from an inconspicuous place, perhaps seated with the audience, as part of the outer circle.

In some places there is action without narration. Here a small group of children can add atmosphere and feeling to the movement with Indian music. Listen to records of Indian singing, and try and create this mood. The music is not easy for adults to sing, but I found when I toured elementary schools with the Eric Nicol's play, *Why the Clam Made a Face* (based on Indian legends) that the children picked up the tunes of the Indian songs very quickly.

You will need two different drums and perhaps a rattle and a flute or recorder. Indian music does not have harmony in the same sense as our music, so you do not need an expert on the flute. A few birdlike notes will be quite appropriate. Put your little orchestra on the side of the circle, not too far from the narrator.

If you like the idea of the Creation of the World as a theme for a mime play, but would like to try some other kind of legend, look at the stories of

. The Incas of Peru. These all use masks. Beautiful stories, very suitable for older grades.

. Eskimo legends. These very imaginative stories use the characters of Snow and Ice, and a female Creator.

. Norse or Icelandic legends have Night and Day gods riding around the sky in a chariot, and a great Giant god, Ymir.

. The Genesis story, perhaps using the Bible.

. African legends, particularly those from the West Coast.

Begin in silence and semi-darkness until the narrator speaks:

IN THE BEGINNING THERE WAS NOTHING, AND MAHEO, THE ALL SPIRIT, LIVED IN THE VOID.

Maheo, *crouched in the center of the circle, comes up slowly and majestically and looks far out into the circle, and then listens intently – and goes back into himself.*

HE LOOKED AROUND HIM BUT THERE WAS NOTHING TO SEE. HE LISTENED, BUT THERE WAS NOTHING TO HEAR. THERE WAS ONLY MAHEO ALONE IN NOTHINGNESS.

Maheo comes up again and moves slowly around the circle, returning to the center for —

BECAUSE OF THE GREATNESS OF HIS POWER, MAHEO WAS NOT LONESOME. HIS BEING WAS A UNIVERSE. BUT AS HE MOVED THROUGH THE MINDLESS TIME OF NOTHINGNESS, IT SEEMED TO MAHEO THAT HIS POWER SHOULD BE PUT TO USE.

Maheo spreads open his arms, and beckons in the **Spirit of Water.**

MAHEO CREATED A GREAT WATER, LIKE A LAKE BUT SALTY.

Music cue as **Spirit of Water** *grows bigger and bigger, swirling around the stage and landing beside Maheo in the center.*

OUT OF THIS SALTY WATER MAHEO KNEW HE COULD BRING ALL LIFE THAT WAS EVER TO BE. THE LAKE ITSELF WAS LIFE, IF MAHEO SO COMMANDED IT. IN THE DARKNESS OF NOTHINGNESS MAHEO COULD FEEL THE COOLNESS OF THE WATER, AND TASTE ON HIS LIPS THE TANG OF THE SALT. "THERE SHOULD BE WATER BEINGS" SAID MAHEO.

Enter the **Fish,** *swimming through the same path created by the* **Spirit of Water.**

AND SO IT WAS. FIRST THE FISH SWIMMING IN THE DEEP WATER. . .

Crab *comes scuttling. This could even be a comic sideways walk, with the crab trying to nip the feet of the audience.*

AND THEN THE CRAB. . .

Enter the **Crawfish.** *Take a look at the way a lobster moves, and try to create that feeling with the arms and legs, as the crawfish travels through the "water."*

AND CRAWFISH, LYING ON THE SAND AND MUD.

Music cue, as the fish interact with one another, and with Maheo.

LET US ALSO CREATE SOMETHING THAT LIVES ON THE WATER, MAHEO THOUGHT.

Enter a beautiful **Snowgoose,** *a proud white masked bird with lovely movements, walking and swimming.*

AND SO IT WAS. FOR NOW THERE WERE SNOWGEESE. . .

Bring in the **Mallard.** *The male has brilliant colors and is a swift and lively swimmer.*

*Adapted from "How the World was Made," from *American Indian Mythology* by Alice Marriott and Carol K. Rachlin. Thomas Y. Crowell Co., Inc. 1968.

AND MALLARDS. . .

> The **Coot** ("silly as a coot") is very gawky in its movement, with large clumsy feet. He has a plain black head and a large white bill.

AND COOTS, LIVING AND SWIMMING ABOUT ON THE WATER'S SUR-
FACE. MAHEO COULD HEAR THE SPLASHING OF THEIR FEET AND THE
FLAPPING OF THEIR WINGS IN THE DARKNESS.

> **Spirit of Light** enters during the following speech, and the whole area becomes brilliantly lit as she does so.

I SHOULD LIKE TO SEE THE THINGS THAT HAVE BEEN CREATED,
MAHEO DECIDED. AND AGAIN, SO IT WAS. LIGHT BEGAN TO GROW
AND SPREAD, FIRST WHITE AND BLEACHED IN THE EAST, THEN
GOLDEN AND STRONG TILL IT FILLED THE MIDDLE OF THE SKY AND
EXTENDED ALL AROUND THE HORIZON.

> **Snowgoose** follows the action of the narration.

THEN THE SNOW GOOSE PADDLED OVER TO WHERE SHE THOUGHT
MAHEO WAS. "I DO NOT SEE YOU, BUT I KNOW THAT YOU EXIST," THE
GOOSE BEGAN CALLING TO MAHEO. "THIS IS GOOD WATER THAT YOU
HAVE MADE, ON WHICH WE LIVE. BUT BIRDS ARE NOT LIKE FISH.
SOMETIMES WE GET TIRED SWIMMING. SOMETIMES WE WOULD LIKE
TO GET OUT OF THE WATER." "THEN FLY," SAID MAHEO, AND HE
WAVED HIS ARMS. . .

> All waterbirds fly. Use as much space as you have available, even flying outside the audience area.

AND ALL THE WATER BIRDS FLEW, SKITTERING ALONG THE SURFACE
OF THE LAKE UNTIL THEY HAD SPEED ENOUGH TO RISE IN THE AIR.
THE SKIES WERE DARKENED WITH THEM. "HOW BEAUTIFUL THEIR
WINGS ARE IN THE LIGHT," MAHEO SAID AS THE BIRDS WHEELED AND
TURNED, AND BECAME LIVING PATTERNS AGAINST THE SKY."

> **Mallard** stops and approaches Maheo.

THE MALLARD WAS THE FIRST TO DROP BACK TO THE SURFACE OF THE
LAKE. "MAHEO," HE SAID, "YOU HAVE MADE US SKY AND LIGHT TO
FLY IN AND YOU HAVE MADE US WATER TO SWIM IN. IT SOUNDS
UNGRATEFUL TO WANT SOMETHING ELSE. YET STILL WE DO. WHEN
WE ARE TIRED OF SWIMMING AND TIRED OF FLYING WE SHOULD LIKE
A DRY SOLID PLACE WHERE WE COULD WALK AND REST. GIVE US A
PLACE TO BUILD OUR NESTS, PLEASE, MAHEO." "SO BE IT," ANSWERED
MAHEO, "BUT TO MAKE SUCH A PLACE I MUST HAVE YOUR HELP, ALL
OF YOU." "TELL US HOW WE CAN HELP YOU," SAID ALL THE WATER
PEOPLES. "WE ARE READY TO DO WHAT YOU SAY."

> **Maheo** gathers in the birds.

MAHEO STRETCHED OUT HIS HAND AND BECKONED. "LET THE BIG-
GEST AND THE SWIFTEST TRY TO FIND LAND FIRST," HE SAID, AND
THE SNOW GOOSE CAME TO HIM."

> **Snowgoose** looks for lands, following directions of the story.

"I AM READY TO TRY," THE SNOWGOOSE SAID, AND SHE DROVE HER-
SELF ALONG THE WATER UNTIL THE WHITE WAKE BEHIND HER GREW

AND GREW TO A SHARP WHITE POINT THAT DROVE HER UP INTO THE AIR AS THE FEATHERS DRIVE AN ARROW. SHE FLEW HIGH INTO THE SKY UNTIL SHE WAS ONLY A DARK SPOT AGAINST THE CLEARNESS OF THE LIGHT. THEN THE GOOSE RETURNED, AND DOWN SHE PLUNGED FASTER THAN ANY ARROW, AND DIVED INTO THE WATER. SHE PIERCED THE SURFACE WITH HER BEAK AS IF IT WERE THE POINT OF A SPEAR. THE SNOW GOOSE WAS GONE A LONG TIME. MAHEO COUNTED TO FOUR FOUR HUNDRED TIMES BEFORE SHE ROSE TO THE SURFACE OF THE WATER AND LAY THERE FLOATING WITH HER BEAK HALF OPEN AS SHE GASPED FOR AIR. "WHAT HAVE YOU BROUGHT US?" MAHEO ASKED HER, AND THE SNOWGOOSE SIGHED SADLY, AND AN-SWERED, "NOTHING, I BROUGHT BACK NOTHING."

*The **Mallard** looks for land, following directions of the story.*

THEN THE MALLARD TRIED IN TURN. HE ROSE UNTIL HE WAS A SPECK AGAINST THE LIGHT, AND TURNED AND DIVED WITH THE SPEED OF A FLASHING ARROW INTO THE WATER. AND HE ROSE WEARILY AND WEARILY ANSWERED "NOTHING" WHEN MAHEO ASKED HIM WHAT HE HAD BROUGHT. AT LAST THERE CAME THE LITTLE COOT, PAD-DLING ACROSS THE SURFACE OF THE WATER VERY QUICKLY, DIPPING HIS HEAD SOMETIMES TO CATCH A TINY FISH, AND SHAKING THE WATER BEADS FROM HIS SCALP LOCK WHENEVER HE ROSE.

*The **Coot** now takes up the hunt. All the birds and fish must give the feeling of moving through water, not air, especially in the part where they are diving or swimming down to the depths.*

"MAHEO," THE LITTLE COOT SAID SOFTLY, "WHEN I PUT MY HEAD BENEATH THE WATER, IT SEEMS TO ME THAT I SEE SOMETHING THERE, FAR BELOW. PERHAPS I CAN SWIM DOWN TO IT. I CAN'T FLY OR DIVE LIKE MY SISTERS AND BROTHERS. ALL I CAN DO IS SWIM." "LITTLE BROTHER," SAID MAHEO, "NO MAN CAN DO MORE THAN HIS BEST, AND I HAVE ASKED FOR THE HELP OF ALL THE WATER PEOPLES. CERTAINLY YOU SHALL TRY. PERHAPS SWIMMING WILL BE BETTER THAN DIVING, AFTER ALL. TRY, LITTLE BROTHER, AND SEE WHAT YOU CAN DO."

"HAH-HO," THE LITTLE COOT SAID, "THANK YOU, MAHEO," AND HE PUT HIS HEAD UNDER THE WATER AND SWAM DOWN AND DOWN AND DOWN AND DOWN UNTIL HE WAS OUT OF SIGHT. THE COOT WAS GONE A LONG, LONG, LONG, LONG TIME. THEN MAHEO AND THE OTHER BIRDS COULD SEE A LITTLE DARK SPOT BENEATH THE WATER'S SURFACE SLOWLY RISING TOWARD THEM. AT LAST THE SPOT BEGAN TO HAVE A SHAPE. STILL IT ROSE AND ROSE AND AT LAST MAHEO AND THE WATER PEOPLES COULD SURELY SEE WHO IT WAS. THE LITTLE COOT WAS SWIMMING UP FROM THE BOTTOM OF THE SALTY LAKE. WHEN THE COOT REACHED THE SURFACE HE STRETCHED HIS CLOSED BEAK UPWARD INTO THE LIGHT, BUT HE DID NOT OPEN IT.

Maheo takes imaginary mud from the beak of the coot. If the coot's mask has a beak that will open it makes this part more effective.

"GIVE ME WHAT YOU HAVE BROUGHT," MAHEO SAID. AND THE COOT LET HIS BEAK FALL OPEN SO A LITTLE BALL OF MUD COULD FALL FROM HIS TONGUE INTO MAHEO'S HAND. "GO, LITTLE BROTHER," MAHEO SAID, "THANK YOU AND MAY WHAT YOU HAVE BROUGHT ALWAYS PROTECT YOU." AND SO IT WAS AND SO IT IS, FOR THE COOT'S FLESH STILL TASTES OF MUD, AND NEITHER MAN NOR ANIMAL WILL EAT A COOT UNLESS THERE IS NOTHING ELSE TO EAT.

Maheo's mime indicates the mud slowly growing.

MAHEO ROLLED THE BALL OF MUD BETWEEN THE PALMS OF HIS HANDS, AND IT BEGAN TO GROW LARGER UNTIL THERE WAS ALMOST TOO MUCH MUD FOR MAHEO TO HOLD. HE LOOKED AROUND FOR A PLACE TO PUT THE MUD BUT THERE WAS NOTHING BUT WATER OR AIR ANYWHERE AROUND HIM. "COME AND HELP ME AGAIN, WATER PEOPLES," MAHEO CALLED. "I MUST PUT THIS MUD SOMEWHERE. ONE OF YOU MUST LET ME PLACE IT ON HIS BACK."

Maheo tries each bird and fish.

ALL THE FISH AND ALL THE OTHER WATER CREATURES CAME SWIMMING TO MAHEO, AND HE TRIED TO FIND THE RIGHT ONE TO CARRY THE MUD. THE FISH WERE TO NARROW, AND THEIR BACK FINS STUCK UP THROUGH THE MUD AND CUT IT TO PIECES. FINALLY ONLY ONE WATER CREATURE WAS LEFT.

Very slowly, enter Grandmother **Turtle**.

"GRANDMOTHER TURTLE," MAHEO SAID. "DO YOU THINK THAT YOU CAN HELP ME?" "I AM VERY OLD AND VERY SLOW, BUT I WILL TRY," THE TURTLE ANSWERED. SHE SWAM OVER TO MAHEO AND HE PILED THE MUD ON HER ROUNDED BACK, UNTIL HE HAD MADE A HILL. UNDER MAHEO'S HANDS THE HILL GREW AND SPREAD AND FLATTENED OUT UNTIL THE GRANDMOTHER TURTLE WAS HIDDEN FROM SIGHT. "SO BE IT," MAHEO SAID. "LET THE EARTH BE KNOWN AS OUR GRANDMOTHER, AND LET THE GRANDMOTHER WHO CARRIES THE EARTH BE THE ONLY BEING WHO IS AT HOME BENEATH THE WATER, OR WITHIN THE EARTH, OR ABOVE THE GROUND." AND SO IT IS. GRANDMOTHER TURTLE AND ALL HER DESCENDANTS MUST WALK VERY SLOWLY FOR THEY CARRY THE WHOLE WEIGHT OF THE WHOLE WORLD AND ALL ITS PEOPLES ON THEIR BACKS.

NOW THERE WAS EARTH AS WELL AS WATER, BUT THE EARTH WAS BARREN. AND MAHEO SAID, "OUR GRANDMOTHER EARTH SHOULD BE FRUITFUL. LET HER BEGIN TO BEAR LIFE."

Music plays as **Spirit of Trees** *grows from tiny seed to large trees.* **Spirit of Grass** *waves gently to the music.* **Spirit of Flowers** *grow from seed and open up to reveal their (masked) faces.* **Spirit of Fruits** *offers fruits to Maheo: apples, berries, etc.*

WHEN MAHEO SAID THAT, TREES AND GRASS SPRANG UP TO BECOME THE GRANDMOTHER'S HAIR. THE FLOWERS BECAME HER BRIGHT ORNAMENTS, AND THE FRUITS WERE THE GIFTS THAT THE EARTH OFFERED BACK TO MAHEO. THE BIRDS CAME TO REST ON HER HANDS

WHEN THEY WERE TIRED, AND THE FISH CAME CLOSE TO HER SIDES. MAHEO LOOKED AT THE EARTH AND HE THOUGHT SHE WAS VERY BEAUTIFUL; THE MOST BEAUTIFUL THING HE HAD MADE SO FAR. SHE SHOULD NOT BE ALONE, MAHEO THOUGHT. LET ME GIVE HER SOMETHING OF MYSELF, SO SHE WILL KNOW THAT I AM NEAR HER AND THAT I LOVE HER. MAHEO REACHED INTO HIS RIGHT SIDE AND PULLED OUT A RIB BONE. HE BREATHED ON THE BONE, AND LAID IT SOFTLY ON THE BOSOM OF THE EARTH.

> The **Man** slowly comes to life. As Maheo breathes life into him, he will go fishing, hunting, eat the fruits, learn to swim and dive. Music played while all of this is being done.

THE BONE MOVED AND STIRRED, STOOD UPRIGHT AND WALKED. THE FIRST MAN HAD COME TO BE.

"HE IS ALONE WITH THE GRANDMOTHER EARTH AS I ONCE WAS ALONE WITH THE VOID," SAID MAHEO. "IT IS NOT GOOD FOR ANYONE TO BE ALONE." SO MAHEO FASHIONED A HUMAN WOMAN FROM HIS LEFT RIB, AND SET HER WITH THE MAN.

> Maheo breathes life into the **Woman,** and the man shows her the fish, the flowers, trees, fruits, ducks and water, and they begin to make a life for themselves, making a fire, cooking, sewing, chopping wood.

THEY WERE HAPPY TOGETHER, AND MAHEO WAS HAPPY AS HE WATCHED THEM.

> Woman brings in a baby (doll) and wraps it Indian style. The man brings her a cradleboard (tickanagan) and the woman puts the baby on her back.

AFTER A YEAR, IN THE SPRINGTIME, THE FIRST CHILD WAS BORN. AS THE YEARS PASSED, THERE WERE OTHER CHILDREN. THEY WENT THEIR WAYS AND FOUNDED MANY TRIBES. THEN MAHEO REALIZED THAT HIS PEOPLE WALKING ON THE EARTH HAD CERTAIN NEEDS, SO HE CREATED ANIMALS TO FEED AND CARE FOR THE PEOPLE.

> Enter **Deer,** and the man goes hunting, killing the deer for food and clothing. The woman makes a fire, they eat meat, and sew together garments.

HE GAVE THEM DEER FOR CLOTHING, AND FOOD, PORCUPINES TO MAKE THEIR ORNAMENTS, AND THE SWIFT HORSES ON THE OPEN PLAINS.

> Enter **Porcupine.** They have a difficult time chasing him (her). Next the encounter between man and **Horse,** and the difficulties of riding the horse, at first.

AT LAST MAHEO THOUGHT TO HIS POWER, "WHY, ONE ANIMAL CAN TAKE THE PLACE OF ALL THE OTHERS PUT TOGETHER." AND THEN HE MADE THE BUFFALO.

> Enter the **Buffalo.** Man and horse go to hunt for the Buffalo, perhaps accompanied by drums.

MAHEO IS STILL WITH US. HE IS EVERYWHERE, WATCHING ALL HIS PEOPLE, AND ALL THE CREATION HE HAS MADE. MAHEO IS ALL GOOD AND ALL LIFE. HE IS THE CREATOR, THE GUARDIAN AND THE TEACHER. WE ARE ALL HERE BECAUSE OF MAHEO.

"THE LIFE OF VIC"

A mime play without masks for older children and teens

CAST
Expandable to a Group of Ten to Twenty

Scene One	Vic	Scene Five	Vic
	Sperm		Factory Workers
	1 Ova		
	Mother	Scene Six	Vic
	Father		Secretary
Scene Two	Vic	Scene Seven	Vic
	Mother		2 Doctors
			3 Nurses
Scene Three	Vic		
	Teacher	Scene Eight	Everyone
	School Children		
Scene Four	Vic		
	Teenagers		
	2 Policemen		

I would like to tell you how this play evolved, with a group of teenagers, in an after school mime class. One boy arrived late one day, complaining bitterly that he had been kept in after school (the usual story): one sinner in the group, so the whole class was kept late as a punishment). "I'm always being kept in places when I really want to leave. That's the story of my life," he said. The discussion that developed from this statement, was the basis for the play. Although the leading role in this play was Vic, the boy who was kept in, it could very easily be adapted to be played by a girl. The presentation was shown to parents, teachers and friends, in the room where we worked — an all-purpose room. At one end of the room there was a screen and we showed eight slides of Vic — at various stages of his life — one for each scene. These were the "titles" for each scene.

As a prologue to this play, Vic himself speaks this poem:

PRAYER BEFORE BIRTH

I am not yet born; O hear me.
Let not the bloodsucking bat or the rat
    or the stoat or the club-footed ghoul
    come near me.

I am not yet born, console me.
I fear that human race may with tall
    walls wall me.
with strong drugs dope me, with wise
    lies lure me
on black racks rack me, in blood-baths
    roll me.

I am not yet born; provide me
With water to dandle me, grass to grow
    for me, trees to talk
to me, sky to sing to me, birds and a
    white light
in the back of my mind to guide me.

I am not yet born; forgive me
For the sins that in me the world shall
    commit, my words
when they speak me, my thoughts when
    they think me,
my treason engendered by traitors be-
    yond me,
my life when they murder by
    means of my
hands, my death when they live me.

I am not yet born; rehearse me
In the parts I must play and the cues I
    must take when

old men lecture me, bureaucrats hector
    me, mountains
frown at me, lovers laugh at me, the
    white
waves call me to folly and the
    desert calls
me to doom and the beggar re-
    fuses
my gift and my children curse
    me.

I am not yet born; O hear me,
Let not the man who is beast or who
    thinks he is God come near me.

I am not yet born; O fill me
With strength against those who would
    freeze my
humanity, would dragoon me into a
    lethal automaton,
would make me a cog in a machine,
    a thing with
one face, a thing, and against all
    those
who would dissipate my entirety,
    would
blow me like thistledown
    hither and
thither or hither and thither
like water held in the
hands would spill me.

Let them not make me a stone and let
    them not spill me.
Otherwise kill me.

LOUIS MACNEICE
(Springboard, 1944)

1. BIRTH OF VIC

Lighting and heartbeat sounds comes up on one girl (the ova) stage center rolled up as small as possible like an egg. She moves just a little, rocking slightly from side to side. Suddenly sperm (as many males as you have available) enter from all four sides and dart about, like tadpoles in water. Eventually all the sperm touch the ova, and all are rejected except one. These two make themselves as small as possible. Lights fade and all exit, except Vic, now an embryo. Enter six girls (they are the walls of the uterus and they surround the embryo completely, arms outstretched to make a wall). The embryo very, very slowly develops into a fetus — eyes closed arms and feet developing, and finally, the fingers and toes. The fetus pushes with his head against the walls of the uterus, and very gradually emerges. As he is born, enter the parents — father with a cigar — the mother with a baby blanket. They are delighted with him and immediately wrap him in a blanket. (The first lock-in). Vic opens his eyes and looks around as the lights fade.

2. VIC AS A BABY

Vic is in his crib (imaginary) on one side of the rectangular playing area.

He wakes up and plays in his crib with imaginary toys. He gets bored and turns for comfort to his blanket. At last his mother comes and lets down the crib and he crawls into the kitchen. The mother makes baby food and straps him in his high chair and feeds him. She takes him out, and he heads for something dangerous. His mother is alarmed, and puts him in the playpen. He cries and has a temper tantrum, and tries to climb out of the playpen. His mother picks him up and wheels in a stroller. Vic stops crying as he is strapped into the stroller, and wheeled around to visit with the audience. (He's been locked in four times).

3. VIC IN SCHOOL

The children enter one by one, including Vic. They line up, and fool around on line (think of all the things children do while waiting on line). The school bell rings; they all enter imaginary doors — up six stairs to a classroom. They sit in rows, open desks, and take out books. The teacher enters and everyone says the Pledge of Allegiance (in mime). The teacher writes on the board and the children copy it. While she is writing, Vic misbehaves. The teacher turns around and catches him, and makes him stand in the corner. The bell rings. All the children are dismissed, except Vic. He has to stay in the corner. The teacher locks the door on him while the other children go outside to play.

The children play hopscotch — tag — marbles — baseball, etc. Eventually, the children leave and Vic is left alone in the classroom as the lights fade.

4. VIC AS A TEENAGER

A group of teens are hanging out on the corner of a street. (What do you suggest they do?) Enter Vic on a motorcycle. He greets the rest of the kids. They all huddle together and Vic takes out a marijuana cigarette. They all pass one around each taking a drag of it. A police siren is heard. Enter a policeman. All the group get away except Vic, who is caught with a cigarette in his hands by the policeman. He is taken to jail. Another policeman opens up the cell and locks him in an imaginary jail. He shakes the bars, feels the walls all around him, but he can't get out; so he just drops to the floor.

5. VIC'S FIRST JOB

An assembly line job. The whole group including Vic are working on an imaginary machine. Decide what kind of a machine you will use, and who operates what. The work should be very repetitive.

The machine gradually gets faster and faster until the chief operator rings a bell and it stops. Everyone takes a break. Most people go to other machines for cigarettes, soda, and coffee. Vic goes to the opposite end of the room, away from the other workers. He opens a window and looks out. He stretches and enjoys the sunlight. A bell rings, and everyone goes back to work with exactly the same mechanical movements as at the beginning. Vic goes through all the motions but keeps his eye on the sunlight through the window.

6. VIC THE EXECUTIVE

Vic enters. He takes a large bunch of keys to open his office door. He checks the clock and his watch and his secretary comes scurrying in behind him — a little late. She sits at the desk and types. The phone rings. Vic is on the telephone and the secretary gets him coffee. He dictates letters (in mime talk) and paces up and down. He goes through papers, checks files, smokes a cigarette, drinks his coffee. All this work is constantly interrupted by the telephone ringing. Vic is almost like a robot going back and forth from the telephone to his desk. He does manage to look out of the window once and relax, feeling the sun on his face, but the telephone rings, and he goes back to being a robot. The pace gets faster and faster — between secretary — file cabinet — desk — ashtray — and telephone (like a film getting speeded up). Vic has a heart attack. The secretary is about to rush to him as the telephone rings. She answers the telephone.

7. VIC IN HOSPITAL

Vic is in bed. He tries to get up to go to the window but he is constantly visited by a stream of doctors, nurses, dietician, volunteers for temperature, meals, magazines, etc. The moment he tries to get out of bed, another person arrives on the scene. Eventually he is left alone. He takes two sheets and with difficulty gets out of bed and goes to the window. He opens it and ties the two sheets together to make an escape rope. He starts to climb down and when he gets to the bottom he jumps — only to be confronted by two nurses and a doctor with a straight jacket. He fights but they win.

8. FINAL SCENE

Of course, the inevitable and last stage, the ultimate "lock-in" is death. If you wish to end the life of Vic with his funeral, then six pallbearers carry in the body of Vic followed by mourners carrying candles and wearing black veils or armbands. Slowly his body is lowered into a grave. A priestly type of figure mutters some incantation (no real words). The grave digger throws earth on the grave and mourners blow out the candles. All the fears of Louis Mac Neice's poem have been realized.

I would prefer to say to anyone contemplating the production of this play — what would be your prayer before death for Vic? How do you want to end the play? Does Vic finally escape and if so, where does he go? Do you want to end the play with a poem or a song as we began? Or will movements say more? If you really cannot decide, or do not wish to, you can always ask your audience to participate. Ask them, "What is Scene 8?"

ACKNOWLEDGEMENTS

In the writing of this book, I have people to thank in several countries:

In England,   Marjorie Judson and Ruth Tyson, who encouraged me early in life;

Rose Bruford, Greta Stevens, and James Dodding, for inspired teaching in mime;

Joan Turner ("Peri"), a great Mime artist and a long-time friend.

In Canada,   David Barnet, with whom I shared many of these ideas;

The late Powys Thomas, an Actor-Teacher, loved and acclaimed by many.

In America,   Paula Silberstein for her friendship and the warm introduction to this book;

Katherine McCabe for her beautiful drawings;

Cindy Pratt and Dorothy Ballou, two teacher friends who shared ideas with me,

Julianna Soos for her contribution to the mask work;

and the Mummenshanz players for joy and inspiration every time I saw them.

Hundreds of students in all three countries, who responded with great imagination and creativity.

Finally, for their patience, enthusiasm, and love, I thank my parents, Edna and Bob Dolby; my husband, Maury, and my three "mime-minded" children — Melissa, Celia, and Paul.

                                        Roberta Nobleman

OHEC.
Brescia
792.3 Nobleman, Roberta.
N753
Mime and masks

DATE			
MR 23 '92			